# Public Service Broadcasting
# without the BBC?

# Public Service Broadcasting without the BBC?

PROFESSOR SIR ALAN PEACOCK

INTRODUCTION BY PHILIP BOOTH

WITH COMMENTARIES BY
DAVID GRAHAM
CAROLYN FAIRBAIRN
ED RICHARDS & CHRIS GILES
STEPHEN PRATTEN & SIMON DEAKIN

The Institute of Economic Affairs

First published in Great Britain in 2004 by
The Institute of Economic Affairs
2 Lord North Street
Westminster
London SW1P 3LB
in association with Profile Books Ltd

The mission of the Institute of Economic Affairs is to improve public understanding of the fundamental institutions of a free society, with particular reference to the role of markets in solving economic and social problems.

A CIP catalogue record for this book is available from the British Library.

ISBN 0 255 36565 9

Many IEA publications are translated into languages other than English or are reprinted. Permission to translate or to reprint should be sought from the Director General at the address above.

Typeset in Stone by MacGuru Ltd
info@macguru.org.uk

Printed and bound in Great Britain by Hobbs the Printers

# CONTENTS

## THE AUTHOR

Alan Peacock has, in his time, been a sailor (1942–5), Professor of Economics in four major universities (1957–84), Chief Economic Adviser to the DTI (1973–6), Principal and then Vice-Chancellor of the independent University of Buckingham (1980–85). He has also been an economic consultant to governments, international agencies and professional bodies. He has spent the last twenty years in 'active retirement' as co-founder of the David Hume Institute, Edinburgh. He has served as chairman of the Home Office Committee on Financing the BBC (1985–6). A fellow of the British Academy and the Royal Society of Edinburgh (Royal Medallist) and an honorary fellow of the London School of Economics and Political Science and of the IEA, Sir Alan has been awarded eleven honorary degrees, including a doctorate from his alma mater, St Andrews. He was awarded a knighthood for public service in 1987.

# FOREWORD

The future of public service broadcasting and the future of the BBC are both under consideration by the government, as it reviews the BBC's charter, and by the regulator Ofcom. As the BBC has particular public service obligations, the future of the BBC and the future of public service broadcasting are currently, of course, inextricably linked.

A key radical theme of the Peacock report into the funding of broadcasting, published in 1986, was that the provision of public service broadcasting could, in the future, be separated from the institution of the BBC. From a practical point of view, Peacock's arguments are even more relevant today than twenty years ago because we have now reached the point at which technology allows Peacock's vision to become a reality. As Peacock envisaged, it is now possible to provide a limited fund, financed by television viewers, that is used to finance the production and broadcasting of programmes that might have some public service value but, for some reason, are not provided in a free market. Correspondingly it would then be possible to finance the BBC by voluntary subscription rather than by a compulsory licence fee.

Now that the theoretical ideal is attainable in practice, there is a challenge to academics, policy-makers and opinion-formers to refine and sharpen their arguments and expose them to public debate. With contributions from Professor Peacock himself and other respected academics in the broadcasting field, from a director of the BBC, from representatives of the regulator Ofcom and from an independent producer, *Public Service Broadcasting without the BBC?* provides an important contribution to the debate on the future of broadcasting policy.

Reform would have ramifications throughout the commercial broadcasting sector. Not only would commercial broadcasters have access to any fund that was set up to subsidise public service broadcasting, but also the implications of a fully commercial BBC, with a dominant market position and access to a huge amount of intellectual property, cannot be ignored. Peacock and the commentators address these issues too. In a new model for financing public service broadcasting, the BBC does not have to have fully commercial objectives: there is plenty of room for imaginative thinking both about the financing of public service broadcasting and about the future corporate structure of the BBC.

Occasional Paper 133 provides an excellent contribution to the debate on the future of broadcasting. This paper resulted from a lecture and discussions on the future of public service broadcasting held at the IEA in cooperation with Ofcom. The IEA would like to thank David Currie and Ed Richards for the part they played in the lecture and discussions. The events were held to promote education on the issue of public service broadcasting among staff from Ofcom, academics, senior management in the broadcasting industry and other interested parties.

The contents of this paper should be regarded as the views of the authors, not as the views of the IEA (which has no corporate view), its managing trustees, Academic Advisory Council or senior staff. The contents of Professor Peacock's paper should also not be regarded as the views of Ofcom or its senior staff.

JOHN BLUNDELL

*Director General,*

*Institute of Economic Affairs*

July 2004

# SUMMARY

- New technology now allows a radically different approach to the provision of public service broadcasting, as anticipated by the 1986 Peacock Report into the funding of the BBC.
- So-called public service broadcasting is currently mainly provided in two ways. First, the BBC receives licence payers' money and free access to spectrum in return for fulfilling 'public service' objectives. Also, public service obligations are imposed upon holders of commercial television franchises.
- There is no longer any technical reason to maintain the current approach to public service broadcasting. That approach, which institutionalises it within particular organisations, such as the BBC, inhibits competition and innovation.
- A limited public service broadcasting fund available on a competitive basis to all broadcasters and producers should be made available. This mechanism would be sufficient to ensure the provision of programmes with 'public service content' that would, perhaps, not be provided in a fully commercial market.
- Such a public service fund would make resources more widely available and would allow the market to adapt to new

technologies and changing views as to the desired content of public service broadcasting.

- There are dangers in continuing to allow the BBC to determine the content of public service broadcasting whilst also delivering the content.
- At the same time as the creation of a public service broadcasting fund, access to the BBC would become voluntary – for example, by subscription.
- The BBC should not be 'privatised' as a fully commercial organisation because its market power and access to intellectual property would create serious competitive distortions.
- Some form of corporate structure should be found for the BBC that allows it to be free and independent but gives it more diverse corporate aims than those held by commercial broadcasters.

# Public Service Broadcasting without the BBC?

# 1 INTRODUCTION
*Philip Booth[1]*

## Background

Throughout the 1980s and 1990s, many industries that had been subject to state control were privatised with substantial benefits accruing to the consumer and the taxpayer. Some industries remained largely inside the public sector, such as postal services – at least with regard to the letters delivery service – and broadcasting. In both these cases, the political involvement in the industries pre-dated the wave of nationalisations in the 30 years following the end of World War II. It could be argued that, at least in the case of broadcasting, technological limitations at the time state involvement began meant that it was more difficult to envisage competitive private markets developing in the provision of services. This particular reason for initiating state involvement in broadcasting has become rather weak in the last decade or so as new technologies have developed and been disseminated. Thus it is important to look rigorously, first, at whether there is still an economic case for state involvement in broadcasting and, second, at the form any state involvement should take.

Professor Sir Alan Peacock anticipated the technological

---

1    Editorial and Programme Director, Institute of Economic Affairs, and Professor of Insurance and Risk Management, Sir John Cass Business School.

developments that would change the face of broadcasting when the Peacock Report into the financing of broadcasting (CFBBC, 1986) was published in 1986. At the current time, the BBC is undergoing a charter review, and Ofcom is undertaking a review of public service broadcasting (see Ofcom, 2004). Thus policy-makers should once again consider the arguments of the Peacock Report, particularly as the timing of the anticipated adoption of technological developments is now clearer than it was in 1986.

## Comments on Peacock's proposals

The monograph begins with Professor Peacock bringing rigorous but lucid economic analysis to bear on the issue of public service broadcasting and the institutional arrangements for its delivery. Peacock introduces his rationale for state intervention in broadcasting with a discussion of consumer sovereignty. Public service broadcasting should consist of supplying consumer wants where such wants, for some reason, cannot be provided through the market. Public service broadcasting should not consist of some self-appointed guardians of the public interest promoting their own views of consumers' interests. Peacock's second working hypothesis is that intervention should be based on the assumption that there is 'workable competition' in the market for broadcasting. Thus we are no longer in the world of spectrum shortage justifying, in the eyes of many, considerable state control of the few television channels to ensure that these limited channels do not all provide programming that attracts the median viewer. Rather we are close to the position where a wide variety of channels can cater for different needs and tastes, including satisfying minority tastes and providing educational programmes and sophisticated current affairs programmes.

The use of the notion of 'workable competition', rather than that of 'perfect competition' coupled with the doctrine of 'market failure', for the backdrop to the analysis is important. As has been noted by Blundell and Robinson (2000) and elsewhere, including recently in reports by the government's own Better Regulation Taskforce, the 'market failure' justification for intervention is seriously problematic. Indeed, the concept of 'market failure', strictly applied, can be regarded as literally vacuous – that is, empty of any meaning. No market can fulfil the conditions for perfect competition and all markets fail relative to that standard. If a market does not meet the conditions then there must be undiscovered opportunities for meeting consumer preferences. But in the absence of perfect competition, we cannot know what those opportunities involve because the information that is necessary to meet them is dispersed among the participants in the market and cannot be centralised. Furthermore, not only does the state not know how to correct market failure but, in doing so, it incurs costs and imposes costs on the market that may be greater than the benefit that could possibly come from addressing the market failure. Also, the government cannot be assumed to work benignly in the interests of market participants but, instead, officials will promote their own interests and the interests of those groups that wield most power in the electoral and lobbying processes.

It is gratifying that Peacock does not use the empty market failure doctrine to justify his position, but it is even more gratifying that Richards and Giles, who work for the broadcasting regulators Ofcom, in their commentary, eschew the market failure doctrine too: their contribution will be discussed in greater detail below.

While Peacock does not use a strict version of the market failure doctrine, he does suggest that intervention mechanisms could be used to provide programmes that consumers want but which are not provided in a market. This may include programmes such as current affairs programmes that people believe should be made available even to those who do not regularly watch them or who are unwilling to pay for them. Peacock's justification for intervention is that there are some forms of programming that consumers as a group may want but which, perhaps because of externalities, are not provided in a free market. Peacock is very careful not to define the extent of such programming that would not be provided in the market. It might be a wide range – sport, cultural programmes, educational programmes, religious programmes, etc. – or it might be a narrow range – for example, just news programmes. Peacock is arguing for a specific mechanism to achieve a specific objective; he does not discuss how widely that mechanism should be used.

If it is the case, as it seems to Peacock, that consumers as a group may want programmes that would not be provided in a market, then it seems logical to develop mechanisms to address this particular problem. The mechanism, argues Peacock, would be to define a sum of money, obtained from a levy on television owners that would be distributed by a body such as an arts council to producers and broadcasters. The make-up of the council would be determined by viewers themselves – it would represent viewers and not be either self-serving or appointed by the government. Peacock does not discuss in detail how the council would use the money allocated to it. But broadcasters and producers could apply for funds to achieve 'public service' aims. The applicants would have to demonstrate that the programmes receiving funding would not be viable on a purely commercial basis. Indeed, the funding could be used in a subtle way, rather like 'restrictive covenants' on a property. If, for example, a particular broadcaster produced a twenty-minute Asian news service each night, the council could pay a small sum of money – much less than the cost of production – in return for certain public service enhancements (say, a commitment not to take more than one minute of advertising, a commitment to a regional version, or a commitment to providing subtitles in Welsh). Thus the council would not just fund the production of whole programmes but might fund public service enhancements to programmes. Of course, there is the problem, anticipated in the commentary by Fairbairn, that the council may end up funding programmes that would have been produced in the private market in any case. The defence against this is that bidding for funds would be a competitive process and it would be a matter for the council to put those funds to the best use, in terms of producing the greatest enhancement to broadcasting to achieve public service aims.

Peacock's proposals have implications for the BBC. It would no longer be special in terms of its role in public service broadcasting. It could still be special as an institution, however. It could obtain its income from a mix of commercial services, subscription and advertising. Peacock believes, however, that if the BBC were made fully commercial it would, in fact, be a serious problem to the competition authorities because of its market power. He suggests that the BBC could be a private, non-profit-making body, rather like the National Trust, with full involvement of subscribers in choosing those who governed the corporation.

One of the main benefits of Peacock's proposals is that they would automatically open the market up to competition. At the moment, the various institutions involved in broadcasting in the UK do rather different things – that is why the range of programming undertaken by satellite channels can, to some people, sometimes seem less imaginative than that produced by the BBC: there is no point in the satellite channels providing exactly what the BBC already provides for free. The benefits of competition could be widespread. Peacock's approach would allow broadcasters to find the optimal degree of vertical integration; it would allow niche broadcasters to compete with the BBC for public service broadcasting funding; it would allow hitherto unforeseen methods of providing better programming to develop which might have been prevented by the existence of one dominant player on the public service broadcasting scene.

## Remarks on the commentaries on Peacock's proposals

Peacock's proposals are then subject to scrutiny by four expert commentators. The first is an independent producer; the second is a BBC executive; the authors of the third commentary work for the regulator Ofcom; and the authors of the fourth commentary are academics.

In the first commentary, David Graham broadly agrees with Peacock. He stresses the importance of competition. Competition is essential if we are to discover new ways of delivering broadcasting and if we are to foster innovation. Graham also comments on the problems of 'government failure' that arise in situations where there is a dominant state provider of a service. He warns against the view that has been adopted by some that the BBC is akin to the National Health Service in providing an essential public service.

Fairbairn, though, issues some strong challenges to Peacock's analysis. Indeed, she does use the NHS analogy when she states, 'In the UK, public service broadcasting is not about narrow market failure, any more than public service health and education are. It is about the collective decision we make as a society to keep some important aspects of our lives in the public realm – available to all, serving all and accountable to all.'

Fairbairn begins by suggesting a number of reasons why the market may fail to provide what consumers want in broadcasting, although it is not clear from her analysis that the Peacock proposals would not address this problem. It matters little, however, whether she believes that they would or not because she does not accept Professor Peacock's framework of thinking. Broadcasting, she argues, holds a special place in society, and it is necessary to have independent, public service institutions that provide a service for the benefit of the public as a whole. Fairbairn suggests that consumer sovereignty subordinates this notion of 'social choice' and the core principles of universality, equity and accountability that underpin it in broadcasting policy.

With regard to the method of funding, Fairbairn argues that using subscription funding for the BBC would undermine the institution because some would choose not to pay, thus raising costs to others, and thus the whole basis of funding for the public service institutions would be eroded: thus licence fee funding is essential.

She suggests that one of the major strengths of the UK's mixed broadcasting system is that the variety of funding sources – subscription, advertising and the licence fee – leads to a variety of content provision. The different content and genre mixes on BBC One as compared with ITV1 or Sky One, it is argued, are testament to this. Interestingly, Fairbairn believes that direct investment by broadcasters in the development of *domestic* content is important – the contribution of the BBC to such investment is mentioned directly no fewer than four times in the commentary. Thus, it would appear, public service broadcasting is not just about output but about the inputs being 'domestic' and the production process being vertically integrated. The institutional aspect of public service broadcasting is important, according to this view.

Fairbairn further argues that the BBC is the 'social glue' that binds the community together and that the BBC is in the best position to make use of a whole range of likely technological developments that can enable the provision of educational services. Peacock's specific proposal for an arts-council-type body is regarded as speculative and untested. She believes that strong institutions are necessary to deliver good public service broadcasting and that programme-based funding for public service broadcasting would crowd out commercial investment as well as undermining accountability, given that the BBC is 'accountable to the British people for the quality of what it does, through a framework of checks and balances'.

Fairbairn's analysis does raise a number of challenges to Peacock. It raises a number of questions too, which are probably best posed in the language of Austrian and public choice economics. First, how does the institution of the BBC know what is in the public interest? Public service broadcasting involves producing and broadcasting programmes that would not be produced directly through producers and broadcasters responding to the information contained in the price signals transmitted by consumers. In the absence of the information arising from such price signals, why is a public institution involved with the production and broadcasting of programmes in a better position than, say, an arts-council-type body to deliver or procure public-service-type programmes? Second, how do we ensure that a public institution fulfils the role that is expected of it? Public choice economics tells us that there is a high probability that it will fulfil a range of other interests instead (those of the unions, the management, the programme producers, the governors, the state, and so on ...). How confident can we be that, in any real sense, the BBC is 'accountable to the British people'? No British person can withdraw their support by not paying the licence fee and not receiving the service. It is also not clear that in quinquennial elections the quality of BBC programming plays a major part in voting decisions.[2, 3]

Fairbairn notes the popularity of the BBC – 94 per cent of people watch it at least once a week. Any other result would be incongruous, however. The BBC receives about £5 billion of public funding: about half from the licence fee and the other half from the value of free spectrum. The BBC has to be paid for by viewers regardless of whether a television owner watches it. Some competitors receive money only from advertising revenue, and others are financed by an extra subscription. It would be strange indeed if the BBC did not provide worthwhile programming with the financial resources at its command. The issue is whether these resources should be available to others on a competitive basis. It would be unfair, however, to criticise Fairbairn for relying on this evidence for the BBC's popularity as there is other evidence cited

---

2   This could be regarded as an unfair suggestion. No doubt Fairbairn would suggest that the checks and balances are much more subtle and involve legal and constitutional (in its widest sense) mechanisms.

3   The BBC has recently produced a document (BBC, 2004) exploring this issue.

both by Fairbairn and also by Richards and Giles that the BBC does, indeed, command public support.

These arguments of public choice economics do not fatally wound the case for the BBC that Fairbairn makes because similar objections could also be directed at Peacock. Will the 'arts council for the air' really represent the consumer interest properly or will it represent the interests of the articulate people who will seek to be its members? The issue of which type of body is best able to fulfil the public service aims and which would be least inclined to pursue its own interests rather than the public interest is a legitimate area for debate. This author's view is that the competitive process that would surround the arts-council-type approach would give this body the edge and that a widening role for the BBC in other areas of education is something that could be regarded as undesirable and an inhibition to genuine intellectual competition. The arts-council-type approach would also foster competition in broadcasting. Furthermore, Peacock hopes that his proposals would not, in fact, lead to the commercialisation of the BBC – a corporation does not have to have commercial aims.

Fairbairn's point about voluntary subscription eroding the licence fee base is also an important one. On the one hand it could be argued that the whole essence of public service broadcasting is that all benefit from it and therefore all should pay. On the other hand, it could be argued that, to justify a compulsory licence fee, one has to prove that those who would choose not to pay the fee would benefit from public service broadcasting to the extent of the fee. This is difficult to prove and, if it were proven, would probably make the case for financing the BBC from general taxation rather than through a licence fee. Peacock believes that there should be a public service levy on all television owners in any case, thus the debate really centres around three questions: How large should the levy be? Should it only be available to the BBC? And how should all the other aspects of the BBC's work – those that do not involve public service broadcasting – be financed? Of course, Fairbairn would argue that the institution is inseparable from the public service ethic and that this provides a strong argument for the status quo.

Regardless of whether one agrees with Fairbairn's position, it is an important defence of the current institutional arrangements. In so far as those who take a different position disagree with it and have to respond to it, it also raises the intellectual quality of the debate, something that can only lead to better decision-making in the Ofcom public service broadcasting review and BBC charter review processes.

In their commentary Richards and Giles accept much of Peacock's economic analysis but implicitly see a wider role for public service broadcasting than does Peacock. They see individuals as both consumers and citizens and believe that there is a case for broadcasting meeting the desires of individuals in both roles. They accept Peacock's argument that the particular way of regulating public service broadcasting in the past has entrenched the position of particular broadcasters and perhaps inhibited technological developments, such as rediffusion, in the post-war period and, more recently, cable and satellite television. But Richards and Giles do also see broadcasting as special and not just as part of the broader education industry. The ability of broadcasters to reach into the homes of so many individuals simultaneously sets it apart as an industry from other aspects of the culture, education and entertainment industries.

Richards and Giles also note that about half of the population still rely on the main terrestrial channels for all their broadcasting consumption. In such circumstances the model of regulating providers of public service broadcasting is still not irrelevant. Nevertheless, as is discussed below, Richards and Giles regard the forthcoming technological changes as important for the future broadcasting policy. The switch to digital television for the population as a whole can change many of the parameters of the debate.

Richards and Giles argue that there are three main questions to be considered. What is the optimal level of public service broadcasting? How much will the market provide without intervention from the state? And how effective can state intervention be in securing these services through funding or through regulation?

They argue that many public service aims can be achieved within the market itself. They also note that, just because the market does not provide all the public service programming that might be regarded as desirable, it does not follow that intervention by the government will improve the situation: they accept and well understand the vacuity of using the market failure argument as an unchallenged argument in favour of intervention. They suggest that many industries operate in a similar situation to the broadcasting industry, where the marginal cost of reaching an extra customer is close to zero. Different industries find their own ways of dealing with these problems, however – for example, through the use of subscription services – and thus this argument itself does not justify intervention.

There is a sense in which Richards and Giles stand between the position taken by Peacock and that of Fairbairn. Richards and Giles accept the case for opening up access to public service funding. But they also believe that there is a case for keeping licence fee funding for the BBC. Whether this would involve additional funds being raised for other public service providers or a diversion of licence fee funding from the BBC is an open question.

Richards and Giles also argue that there is a time dimension to the question of the financing of public service broadcasting. In particular they make a very perceptive point about how the justification for intervention weakens as competition increases. This is not just because increased competition may lead to more programmes with a public service dimension being provided by the market – including by not-for-profit organisations – but also because it may simply be impossible for governments to procure programmes meeting public service objectives that reach a worthwhile audience at a reasonable cost. Richards and Giles believe that a high priority should be given to the switch-over to digital as this will enhance competition.

Ofcom is continuing its work on public service broadcasting and it is clear that rigorous economic analysis will be at the heart of its investigations into the future of broadcasting regulation. Richards and Giles do not share all Peacock's conclusions but there are many common threads in their analysis of broadcasting markets and the role of the state in facilitating public service broadcasting.

Pratten and Deakin also find it helpful to distinguish between the role of individuals as consumers and their role as citizens. If we accept this distinction then there may be issues of universality and quality that need to be addressed and yet are not addressed in a market that only serves individuals in their role as consumers. They suggest that regulation has two distinct functions – the first is to ensure that the consumer is protected in his role as consumer; the second is to ensure that the social purposes of broadcasting are fulfilled. The market is likely to be the most effective way to achieve consumer satisfaction and may be the most effective way to meet the broader social purposes too. We must at least leave open the possibility, however, that non-private institutions (such as the BBC) may have evolved in such a way, in certain circumstances, that they are able to meet the wider social needs more effectively. The case needs to be argued and the evidence presented, for and against this position.

Pratten and Deakin refer to the 1962 Pilkington Report on broadcasting, which was distinctly paternalist in tone. Ideas such as subscription and commercial television were known to be possible at that time but the Pilkington Report did not necessarily regard them as desirable. The report was strongly criticised by Coase and other economists. At a much later date, the Peacock Report (CFBBC, 1986) brought some sober economic analysis to the debate on public service broadcasting but, Pratten and Deakin note, did not jettison the idea of wider social purposes of broadcasting.

This commentary then discusses how Ofcom is attempting to rise to the challenge that was set by Coase and then by Peacock by attempting to put some value on the social purposes of broadcasting. But this is, of course, impossible to do objectively because the social objectives of broadcasting, as they are defined, are those objectives that cannot be delivered in a market. If that is the case, we have no information on the costs and value of such broadcasting – price signals do not figure in our information set. Other methods of attempting to compute the value of goods that have wider social benefits, such as the use of surveys, etc., are notoriously unreliable.

Pratten and Deakin conclude that common sense dictates

that the needs of the public as consumers should be given priority by broadcasting policy-makers in the modern world but that the onus is still on those who accept this point of view to make the case more convincingly.

The authors of this IEA Occasional Paper bring out the important economic issues that must be considered by those involved with broadcasting policy rigorously but lucidly. The stage is set by Professor Peacock, who, as all the commentators would accept, raised the level of the economic debate when the Peacock Report was published nearly twenty years ago. The commentators, from their different perspectives, have responded to make the text as a whole an important contribution to the analysis of the role of public service broadcasting and the future of the BBC. With regard to the question posed by the title of this monograph, all the authors are clear that the BBC has an important contribution to the future of British broadcasting. The proposals of the main author, Professor Peacock, however, would certainly lead to a very different future for the BBC. It would be a future free of government constraints – except those that relate to all broadcasters – but, in Peacock's view, the BBC should not be fully commercial. Instead, it could borrow aspects from many of the excellent models of corporate structure that have existed in the UK used by corporations whose ends have been only partially commercial.

## References

BBC (2004), *Building Public Value: renewing the BBC for a digital world*, London: BBC Media Centre.

Blundell, J. and C. Robinson (2000), *Regulation without the State*

... *The Debate Continues*, IEA Readings 52, London: Institute of Economic Affairs.

CFBBC (1986), *Report of the Committee on the Financing of the BBC*, Cmnd. 9824, London: HMSO (the Peacock Report).

Ofcom (2004), *Is Television Special?*, <http://ofcom.org.uk>.

## 2 PUBLIC SERVICE BROADCASTING WITHOUT THE BBC?

*Professor Sir Alan Peacock*

### Preamble

This paper arises from a lecture given at the Institute of Economic Affairs on 28 January 2004 that was hosted jointly by the IEA and Ofcom. I am grateful to the IEA and Ofcom for the opportunity to deliver that lecture and for the interesting discussions that ensued. It is a development of ideas that have been promoted in a number of the author's previous discussions of broadcasting economics and policy. These include: 'The political economy of public service broadcasting' in his book *The Political Economy of Freedom* (Edward Elgar, 1997) and 'Market failure and government failure in broadcasting', *Economic Affairs* (Institute of Economic Affairs, December 2000). The article in *Economic Affairs* is the editorial introduction to a symposium on 'The Future of Broadcasting' which includes David Graham's discussion of alternatives to conventional broadcasting transmission mentioned in the above text.

Like all writers on the political economy of broadcasting, I owe an immense debt to Ronnie Coase, my senior colleague at the LSE in my salad days, who published his now famous *The British Broadcasting Corporation: A Study in Monopoly* (Bell for the London School of Economics and Economic Science, 1950) when the penetration of economics into the workings of hallowed public institutions was regarded almost as a cardinal sin. That work embodies an earlier study published in *Economica* (August 1948) on the history of 'wire broadcasting' in Britain which is a fascinating story of the onslaught of officialdom, at that time worried that independent initiatives in improving access to broadcasting services would result in the corruption of public morals. How things have changed!

Clearly I write from a liberalist perspective although I argue that a counter-thesis requires the adoption of different value judgements from mine. I recommend particularly Andrew Graham and Gavyn Davies's *Broadcasting, Society and Policy in the Multimedia Age* (University of Luton Press, 1997), all the more interesting because of the subsequent careers of the authors as Master of Balliol, and a well-known adviser to the Labour Party and until recently Chairman of the BBC Governors, respectively.

Several of the basic ideas in the paper are contained in the *Report of the Committee on the Financing of the BBC* (CFBBC, 1986), particularly its final chapter on conclusions and recommendations. As chairman I owe an immense debt to all members of the committee and to Dr Robert Eagle, our secretary. In the subsequent debate on the analytical and policy issues the committee raised, which still continues, I have particularly enjoyed my discussions with and the separate writings of Samuel Brittain, but although we are in profound agreement, I believe, on fundamental issues, he might take a rather different view about the timing of changes in broadcasting structure, especially in regard to the position of the BBC. But he is his own man and knows his own mind!

Finally I should mention and comment on *Beyond the Charter*, the report of the Broadcasting Policy Group of the Conservative Party, chaired by David Elstein, which appeared shortly after this lecture was delivered. It is a serious and important contribution to the debate on the future of the BBC but I must confess to experiencing, I suspect along with other members of the Home Office committee, a strong element of déjà vu in their presentation of the main arguments for adapting the broadcasting system, and particularly the BBC, to the requirement that it should be designed to conform to the public's own assessment of their cultural interests. A curious feature of the report is the oblique references to the role of our committee in which it is implied that we were the passive recipients of fresh thinking on the future structure of the broadcasting system instead of its originators! Nevertheless, it is particularly welcome because it is able, in the light of technological changes and changes in public attitudes since we reported, to fill out the institutional changes needed to implement the continuation and improvement in our system of public service broadcasting. In doing so,the group has challenged the conventional wisdom that the BBC should continue to have special access to public funding. At the same time, *Beyond the Charter* does not follow its own logic to the extent of permitting the BBC to include advertising as a source of revenue.

## Introduction

This paper requires that a value judgement be made about the aim of public service broadcasting. This subject merits some close thinking as a pre-condition for determining what policy action might be taken. The value judgement states that such policy action can only be derived from the tastes and preferences of 'guardians' of the public interest or of individuals in their capacity as purchasers of broadcasting services. Additionally, a judgement made here is that any public action to influence the broadcasting system must accord with the aim of ensuring consumer sovereignty. This means that such action must be derived from the wishes of individuals and that the 'guardians' of the public interest are there to implement those wishes if, for some reason, they are not satisfied in the broadcasting market, and not to impose preferences of their own upon consumers. Therefore 'the interests' of consumers are coterminous with consumer sovereignty. This has important implications for the delivery of broadcasting services, particularly in respect of the creation of a broadcasting 'market'. It will be argued that giving effect to consumer preferences does not require it to be assumed that such preferences are fixed and immutable – a common assumption in welfare economics. Nor does it require that public intervention need only be directed towards removing market failure. A case will be made for some public financing of broadcasting services, subject to safeguards against government failure (see below).

In this paper, I concentrate primarily on television services. Consumer sovereignty requires that a broadcasting market exists that enables consumer preferences to be directly expressed through the market. There is considerable speculation about whether our system will move towards such a situation and how quickly. I will assume that the technical barriers to charging consumers directly for broadcasting are largely disappearing and that competition policy can take care of the promotion of contestability in the markets for broadcasting and programming. There remains the problem of the compatibility of financing by advertising, but, while this creates market imperfections, it is regarded as insufficient to act as a formidable barrier to consumer choice. This allows us to concentrate on the rationale of positive action to promote public service broadcasting through support of those programmes which cannot be provided in the desired amount and balance by direct purchase. The arguments for such action and the form it might take are discussed below.

At present, the most obvious form of direct support for public service broadcasting is through the protection of the BBC from market forces brought about largely by the licence fee and by it being regulated independently of the rest of the broadcasting system. I argue that assigning this function solely to the BBC, as well as relying on the conditions attached to the award of franchises as a method for inducing commercial companies to comply with public service requirements, runs counter to the aim of promoting consumer sovereignty. Substantial modification in the financing of the BBC, however, in order to extend support for public service broadcasting to programming by commercial companies, then raises questions about the rationale for the BBC remaining a public utility, and thus not required to respond to consumer choice exercised through direct payment, and separately regulated by a board of governors. The onus of proof is then placed on government to show that the consumer interest is best achieved other than by the choices of listeners and viewers themselves, as argued below.

## Consumer sovereignty and the market

There are two preliminary points to be made about the relation between consumer sovereignty and the design of broadcasting systems. The first is that the starting point for judging their design by whether they adhere to the principle of consumer sovereignty is a value judgement, and the fact that there is remarkable consensus amongst economists as to the importance of consumer sovereignty, or at least its usefulness as a starting point for welfare analysis, does not denote by itself some technical superiority. This also applies to value judgements that reject consumer sovereignty, however: notably the value judgements of those who believe that broadcasting expertise is to be afforded some special status in the appraisal of the management of the system. We should always be suspicious of those who claim the right to be judges in their own case, and particularly if they make the additional claim that they are the guardians of the public interest. The second is that one must avoid the pitfall of not comparing like with like when it comes to proposals for change in institutional arrangements. One can argue that the consumer sovereignty objective may imply public intervention in the broadcasting market extending beyond that found in other media, but the extent to which this is satisfactory depends on the degree to which government failure can be avoided.

A common practice in economics is to set out the market conditions necessary to accord with consumer sovereignty by reference to welfare economics, where the optimum is achieved by perfectly competitive markets forming a static general equilibrium solution. This approach has its uses, if only to clarify analytical assumptions. Consumers have fixed preference scales and express their choices by purchasing goods and services reflecting their valuation of the alternative uses of their resources. The existence of many buyers and sellers ensures that competition prevails, leading producers to offer goods and services at the lowest prices compatible with remaining in business. Goods and services are divisible in amount and consumers have access to them only if they are prepared to pay. The function of competition is to ensure that producers have an incentive to minimise cost and to provide accurate information to consumers. There are no externalities arising from the actions of consumers or producers.

The derivation of public action using such a model is found by examining whether the assumptions are realistic. Thus perfect competition is prevented by both institutional and technical constraints. It is taken for granted that governments have property rights in the radio spectrum which, until recently, implied that there is some technical limit to the number of broadcasting channels. Such a limitation was compounded by the inability of stations to deny access to those watching their programmes. In any case, with economies of scale in programming the cost of adding an extra consumer, once a programme is made available, becomes zero and charging would violate the welfare rule of equating price and marginal cost. Advertising revenue would not save private provision compatible with the rule because advertisers would wish to maximise audiences and not the welfare of consumers.

According to this model, state action becomes necessary to control entry into broadcasting, because of interference between radio signals, and in order to follow the pricing rule. There are additional if less clear-cut arguments deployed to attack TV and radio advertising on the grounds that maximising audience size reduces programme quality and could have subliminal effects that distort consumer preferences. These consequences have led to campaigns to regulate and to tax such advertising. Finally, the possibility that non-commercial but private broadcasters could overcome the problems of not being able to charge individuals and of providing programmes desired by their consumers by voluntary subscription is largely dismissed because these would be either only limited in their operation or liable to fail because free riders could not be prevented from enjoying their products.

This model introduces a systematic bias in favour of state intervention. A static approach with competitive equilibrium as the norm ignores the important fact that it is the very existence of disequilibrium which indicates to entrepreneurs that there may be opportunities to make more than normal long-run profits, encouraging them to use process and product innovations to improve such prospects. In the context of broadcasting, this could include ways of eroding government influence in the market by legal means, such as through new methods of transmission. An interesting historical example from the 1920s and 1930s, which we owe to the Nobel laureate Ronald Coase, is 'rediffusion', whereby radio programmes could be sent by wire from one receiver to customers with only an extension speaker so that they did not need to buy a radio set. Despite the process being cheaper and with the benefit of better reception, the innovator and his successor were made to operate under strict government regulation designed to protect the interests of the radio industry and the BBC monopoly. It is reasonable to suppose that developments in cable transmission would have occurred much earlier but for this regulatory regime. Thus, there is a danger that government intervention in an 'imperfect' market will actually prevent the innovation that can bring about a greater degree of competition.

The adoption of a purist position on the nature of competition, instead of the acceptance of the objective of 'workable competition', also encourages the belief that broadcasting should be operated as a public utility, but with the complication that, charging for services being neither possible nor desirable, such a service would need public financing or some arbitrary levy unrelated to the use made of the service by individual listeners and viewers. Whatever results might be achieved in order to improve allocative efficiency must be offset by the problem of ensuring that the proper control measures are in place to minimise costs. Government failure often arises from the difficulties of acting as the principal controlling agent not subjected to the discipline of the market and with the strong possibility that the agent can benefit from its situation as the sole direct source of information about its activities.

A cardinal feature of the concept of workable competition emphasises that entrepreneurs envisage profitable opportunities in enticing consumers to buy new products rather than assuming that their tastes will remain fixed. This discovery process applies also to consumers themselves, whose growing experience of programmes can bring about a reconsideration of their allocation of time between them, and encourage them to invest in information that can aid their choices. Of course, it is difficult for programme providers and broadcasting companies in the commercial sector to take chances on extending their horizons given the attraction of mass-market, short-term returns from advertising revenue, though the growth of subscription and pay-per-view services may offer more opportunities for product differentiation based on new ideas. Nevertheless, it is widely accepted by consumers themselves that there are programmes that they wish to support but which they cannot expect to be provided by purely commercial operations.

Delineation of such programmes accords well with the public service broadcasting definition which governs the BBC's claim that it is there to 'inform, entertain and educate' listeners and viewers. What is at issue is how to give content to this rubric and, if it is accepted, who should decide content and how it should be financed. The principle of consumer sovereignty offers guidance here, for it prescribes that it must be derived as far as possible from the preferences of listeners and viewers. Put in general form, there is likely to be wide support for cultural and educational programmes from which many listeners and viewers feel they derive a benefit although they do not necessarily listen to or watch them. An obvious example is programmes designed to encourage an interest in current affairs so that those who experience them are better informed about matters that may call for their decision as voters, conferring, as is commonly believed, an uncovenanted benefit on others.

There is an inherent difficulty in providing such a service. In a market system, everyone buys the amount of it that they wish at the prevailing price, but this is not possible if the service is indivisible. Once it is provided it is available for all to enjoy whether they are prepared to pay or not. This encourages people not to reveal their true preferences, but if there is escape for one there can be escape for all and the service cannot be financed through the market system. It is possible to conceive of a voluntary solution, but the costs of negotiating agreement on its price and the amount provided, which would rise progressively with the number of possible beneficiaries, can be prohibitive. Thus even a commitment to designing a system that conforms with the consumer sovereignty objective points towards an agreement by which viewers and listeners accept that these difficulties have to be overcome by compulsory means. There may need to be some government intervention to ensure the provision of programmes that may not be provided by broadcasters in a market, where finance is from viewer charges and advertising. But if there is to be some intervention to try to ensure programming in accordance with the consumer sovereignty principle, we then have the public choice problem which recognises that government action itself is not necessarily benign and that those acting on behalf of government do not have perfect knowledge. So, the consumer sovereignty principle then needs to be extended to the public choice problem of how compulsion to finance certain types of programming can be exercised in such a way as to accord with consumer choices, with allocational efficiency being matched by production efficiency in the way public funding is used.

## The case for public funding

In developing a case for public funding, the first requirement is that one has a clear idea of pre-conditions:

(i) The broadcasting system will move towards a situation where workable competition is a reality. The public interest in such matters as suitability of content of programmes, prevention of monopolistic attempts that restrict choice, and so on, will be taken care of by the regulatory system.

(ii) In order to ensure that consumer sovereignty requires public support, channels must be specified which are obliged to contain public service broadcasts. At present the obvious candidates are the main terrestrial channels, but consumer sovereignty itself may suggest that radical changes could take place in broadcasting provision, particularly if the position of the BBC remaining as a public corporation is called into question. In the future, bids for public service broadcasting funding could be supplemented by bids for public funding from cable and satellite channels.

(iii) Depending on one's point of view, public service broadcasting is not the sole or necessarily the most important way of offering individuals the opportunity to develop their wider interests. This is particularly the case so far as products of the creative and performing arts and heritage are concerned, in which there is a well-established tradition of public funding and strong vested interests in protecting it. (In my experience as a member of two arts councils, the idea of public funding in these areas being consumer driven is not one that appeals to cognoscenti who claim to know what is good for us!) Those who assign a special role to broadcasting to promote the public good should be chary about the use of public funding from general taxation, in competition with other claimants on government finance, rather than using some independent source of funds.

The view advanced here assumes that the present system of securing the public service aim is unsatisfactory. This system involves the financing of the BBC largely through the licence fee, with the Board of Governors, as its regulator, giving an assurance that public service aims are met, with the addition of private companies who are awarded a franchise with their performance with regard to public service aims being regulated by Ofcom. Given that private companies will continue to provide a major proportion of transmissions by radio and TV, this arrangement would not be appropriate. I consider that the strictures of the Committee on Financing the BBC, which I chaired, are valid, namely that 'public intervention should be of a positive kind and transparent, to help finance additional production, rather than of a negative, censorious kind, oblique and undetectable, which even the best system of regulation risks becoming' (CFBBC, 1986: para. 566).

## A reformed system of finance

An outline of a reformed system of public service broadcasting financing might look like this. There would be a separate budget to be allocated to programmes that conform with the stated aims of public service broadcasting as translated into a list of approved types of TV productions. Competitive bids would emanate from companies obliged to offer public service broadcasting programmes and these could be made in conjunction with independent producers of programmes. The budget would be financed by a reformed licence fee, i.e. the revenue would be hypothecated as at present but the proceeds would not be for the exclusive use of the BBC. The decisions would be taken by an appointed council with half of its members representing viewers and listeners. The council would also be responsible for monitoring projects and providing full information in an annual report on the extent to which individual project targets were met. This would be another quango, but with the added twist that those who finance it will have a definite say in its operation and decisions.

Any such scheme will have bugs to be worked out of it and this one is no exception. It is easy to argue that all the economist needs do is to solve the conceptual problem and leave the sordid details of implementation to practised administrators. I deplore this attitude and think that we have a responsibility at least to help them not only in specifying aims but also in trying to devise the path along which one must proceed to achieve them. So here is an attempt to look the difficulties in the face even if we then must simply pass them by.

The first question arising is how to determine the amount and composition of the Public Service Broadcasting Fund. In the world of the Department for Culture, Media and Sport, the amount is arbitrary and will reflect the political bargaining process within and between departments and HM Treasury. Hypothecation with user representation on the council, however, creates a more interesting situation, rather as in the case of the national lottery. Probably there will have to be some overall upper limit on the amount of funding and its growth, which would have to be fixed by government in the light of its overall commitment to the finance of cultural activities, leaving the council to decide on its distribution. A degree of flexibility could be introduced by a growth formula related in some way to the growth in overall broadcasting revenue.

The second question is how to meet the general objections to subsidies to particular industries. These are well documented in the economics literature and need no elaboration here. Most of them concern the devising of performance indicators and how they are to be traded off against one another, and the information costs in tracking their movements. The additional difficulty with the content of public service broadcasting will be the perpetual disagreement about what is meant by quality of performance, how to measure it and whose advice should be sought on such matters.

The third question is why one should concentrate on this form of financial provision for subsidising the producers and broadcasters, given the inherent problems. Are there not alternative methods which are simpler, cheaper and more effective?

CFBBC did consider this matter in some detail in respect of a wholly commercialised but regulated system, as in the USA. It has to be recognised that the public role of the US system is primarily to conform with the clauses of the Constitution covering individual liberty, particularly freedom of speech, and cannot be judged in terms of criteria that place emphasis on a collective interest, using broadcasting to improve understanding of important national issues. A commercial approach need not militate against the presentation of programmes beyond the provision of 'enjoyable rubbish' (to quote Lord Quinton, one of the members of CFBBC), as, for example, the encouragement given in the USA to public service broadcasting stations dependent on voluntary subscription and donations which produce our equivalent of cultural programmes. But, nearly two decades after CFBBC was published, the British system has moved to an unexpected degree towards diversity of delivery services and a rapidity of expansion of channels relying on subscription and pay-per-view and not purely on advertising revenue. One should therefore not rule out the alternative of relying on regulation in order to direct the broadcasting system towards meeting the aims of public service broadcasting. This would mean, however, that the regulatory system would have to be extended to cover this function in respect of all broadcasters, including the BBC. The scepticism of CFBBC about the negative nature of regulation (see above) would remain. It would also need to be a system that would have to pay particular attention to what is often a missing element in standard welfare economics as applied to broadcasting, namely the importance of freedom of entry in order to maintain the impetus towards innovation and the opportunity to present consumers with an expansion in choice.

It would be more in line with the philosophy underlying my proposals if some method were found for supporting consumers rather than producers. A voucher scheme might be devised which funded consumers to buy public service broadcasting programmes of their choice. This would mean consumers of programmes being provided with a card for insertion into a receiver, allowing a given number of hours of public service broadcasting viewing. A pre-condition for such a system would be that broadcasting had made a substantial move towards a system of direct payment for individual programmes. It would have to take account of such complications as the growth of self-service TV, as with choices of films, and the prospect that viewers will more and more buy directly from independent producers. It has even been claimed by David Graham (author of the first commentary) that such new methods of programme delivery may allow us to dispense with conventional TV altogether! Of course, unlike with schemes for school vouchers, where the product is compulsorily consumed, there is no compulsion on people to use a voucher card and watch a certain number of hours of public service broadcasting! The system would be more akin to a voucher system for museums, whereby, instead of making museums free at the point of entry, with all the difficulties of determining which museums should benefit, the inefficiencies that arise from abolishing prices, and so on, individuals – particularly parents – are given vouchers that can be exchanged for entry into a wide range of cultural activities. Such vouchers could be used or disposed of.

The difficulty that would have to be faced would be that a market for vouchers could develop in which 'culture vultures' could increase their hours of free viewing by buying – no doubt at a discount – the cards of the 'philistines'. Again, this could happen in a more general voucher system for cultural activities.

A voucher scheme to promote public service broadcasting is unlikely to attract much further immediate investigation. Nevertheless, the history of economic thought and policy, as I know from personal experience, is strewn with examples of what are regarded as bizarre ideas by one generation but are taken up by the next.

## Public service broadcasting and the future of the BBC

The scheme outlined for the implementation of a public service broadcasting system based on consumer sovereignty has important implications for the future of the BBC. It would be wholly inconsistent with the aim of these proposals to continue a system by which the BBC funding of public service broadcasting is obtained from the licence fee, with the main commercial channels obliged, as a condition of their franchises, to follow public service broadcasting rules and raise the finance themselves, with the important 'fringe' of new commercial channels having no such obligation.

The principle of workable competition extends to uniformity of regulation designed to prescribe the minimum public service broadcasting requirements for nationally available TV channels, and, if a case for public funding of public service broadcasting is accepted, that finance should be available to all those faced with such an obligation and on a competitive basis. Particular attention needs to be paid to the position of creators of public-service-type programming and therefore to the claims of independent producers to be included in such a system. This is particularly true if, as is claimed, viewers and listeners become increasingly active in programme selection and in the use of videos for home entertainment and education.

The aim of consumer sovereignty and its implementation with public support removes the case for retaining the BBC as a publicly financed public corporation. Otherwise one perpetuates a system wherein the BBC is judge in its own case as to what public service broadcasting means, and one in which unfair competition prevails in the ability of the BBC to offer highly subsidised commercial services made possible by, amongst other things, the property rights of the BBC in recorded programmes financed by payers of the licence fee.

The desirability of introducing such a radical change is bound to be questioned. Privatisation could take many forms, however, and need not be introduced at one fell swoop. I have suggested elsewhere that the BBC might become a private non-profit-making corporation like the National Trust, perhaps with restrictions on the percentage of its funding that it could raise from commercial activities and encouragement given to support from individual and corporate subscribers who would have voting rights in the election of its governing body. While the licence fee would remain as the source of public service funding, its reduction to the appropriate level could take time, so that the entry of the BBC into the market system would be a gradual process. This might also allay the fears of the broadcasting market incumbents who, while extolling the virtues of competition and consumer sovereignty, understandably do not want the door into their back yard opened too widely and too quickly.

A subtle attack on the 'liberalising' approach to achieving consumer sovereignty objectives questions whether the outcome would conform to the wishes of the public. The very argument that arrangements other than the free market are necessary to take account of the public service dimension in broadcasting could be used to support the position that freedom of choice extends to the methods of choice themselves, and that the public may prefer the present balance in the structure of television provision rather than undergo the risks of change, although this does necessarily mean contentment with the status quo. Public preferences, it is argued, can be taken care of through the system of political representation.

But it would be difficult to argue that the sensitivities of consumers can be as fully reflected in our political system as in properly working markets. The evidence for this lies in the alternative method of political participation found particularly in a centralised system such as ours, namely the organisation of pressure groups seeking official recognition. It may suit broadcasters to recognise particular consumer pressure groups as representative of public opinion and to offer them special status in consultation, but there is no guarantee that their agendas fully reflect that opinion. It would be to move far outside our own agenda to speculate on what changes in modes of political representation provide the best analogue to free consumer choice in markets. It is a moot point whether or not the issue of BBC privatisation in whole or in part will be taken to merit a properly conducted referendum with full opportunity for public discussion beforehand.

There remains a respectable argument for the view that the cultural aspirations of consumers presuppose that there is a general wish to preserve a national culture and the moral values of mutual trust and respect which cannot be supplied by individuals without mutual cooperation. It is claimed by no less a figure than the former Chairman of the BBC, Gavyn Davies, that, given the pivotal role played by television in our ordinary lives, the BBC is the broadcaster best placed to undertake the special task of preserving our national identity and self-esteem as a pre-condition for the preservation of our system of values. This assumes, however, that its independence is assured, and that this goal cannot be effected by making it dependent on the market, perhaps tempered with public funding of public service broadcasting. Furthermore, this is how the BBC is perceived by viewers and listeners all over the world, and this alone offers it a special place in the preservation of our international prestige. It is an argument that I find persuasive in the case of serious radio programmes that by their very familiarity and high standards of integrity have maintained a large following.[1]

This argument can be addressed and its refutation is an important aspect of the case for a new way of financing public service broadcasting. As I have argued in a previous essay:[2]

> the fostering of the qualities which forge a nation's character and influence and which are generally respected, such as enterprise, inventiveness, tolerance and justice, is hardly the function of a broadcasting system, rather it is the function of the educational system in the widest sense. The taste of viewers and listeners is a reflection of these qualities and at most broadcasting is one source of knowledge and should not be raised to the status of a Church, however broad and accommodating its presentation of moral and cultural values may be. Even if it is conceded that there is a public

---

1   My father, Alexander David Peacock, was a pioneer in schools broadcasting, but more than filial piety makes me say this.

2   Peacock (1997: 312).

interest in raising the understanding of a nation's own cultural diversity and the threats it may face from cheap access to the trivialities of Tinseltown, this does not make the case for confining state financial support to a single, monolithic supplier of public service broadcasting.

So to answer the question posed at the beginning of the essay, I do not believe in 'public service broadcasting without the BBC'. But I do believe that a very different method of financing public service broadcasting is necessary. This should be combined with the creation of a very different kind of corporate model for the BBC – neither government-controlled nor fully commercial. Examples of such models have served us well in Britain, in other sectors, over the last two centuries, and continue to do so today.

## References

CFBBC (1986), *Report of the Committee on the Financing of the BBC*, Cmnd. 9824, London: HMSO (the Peacock Report).

Graham, A. and G. Davies (1997), *Broadcasting, Society and Policy in the Multimedia Age*, Luton: University of Luton Press.

Peacock, A. (1997), 'The Political Economy of Public Service Broadcasting', in *The Political Economy of Economic Freedom*, Cheltenham: Edward Elgar.

# 3 COMMENTARY: THE IMPORTANCE OF COMPETITION

*David Graham[1]*

Professor Peacock has made an important contribution and I wholly agree with the foundations of his argument. His starting point is that any public action to influence the broadcasting system must accord with the aim of ensuring consumer sovereignty. The 'guardians' are there to 'implement those wishes' and not to 'impose preferences of their own'. In other words, any intervention by the government should have the support of the viewing population. Peacock acknowledges that determining the wishes of the viewing population is not a simple matter. Referendums on broadcasting policy would be inappropriate. I guess that he might accept well-conducted surveys to determine the types of intervention supported by consumers. He does not question whether consumers currently support such intervention but appears to make the assumption that they do. In this he is probably correct. On the basis of surveys that have been conducted, though their methodology could be improved, consumers accept that the state should ensure high-quality news and information programmes, and – though getting a lower level of support – education and children's programmes. The same surveys do not reveal anything like that level of support

---

1     Chairman of David Graham Associates, a media research company. David was awarded the Royal Television Society medal for Oustanding Services to Television in 2000.

for other currently mandated 'public service genres' such as religious and regional programmes.

Peacock is against any system or structure of intervention that embodies a 'static approach' with competitive equilibrium regarded as the norm, for it ignores the very fact that it is *disequilibrium* which stimulates innovation. Equally important is the preservation of space for new entrants and new ways of providing broadcasting. While any intervention in the market, such as the imposition of public service broadcasting obligations, distorts a market, it must still seek 'workable competition' within that framework. Competition in the supply of public service broadcasting is just as important as competition in any other field and essential for delivering both value for money and innovation. A key point is that neither the 'market' nor consumer tastes are static. A policy guided by consumer sovereignty must offer the flexibility to detect and accommodate change.

It is for these reasons that Peacock argues that the system we have currently does not meet these criteria at all. The BBC, as the sole repository of hypothecated public funding, defines public service broadcasting more or less as it chooses, allocating a large amount of the money it controls to programmes that consumers would be perfectly happy to pay for in their own right. A sole provider, funded by public subsidy, is always a problem: 'we should always be suspicious of those who claim the right to be judges in their own case and, particularly, if they make the additional claim that they are the guardians of the public interest'. Furthermore, the extent to which consumer sovereignty can be satisfactorily implemented depends on 'the degree to which government failure can be avoided'. Government authorises such expenditure, yet it is prone to failure through lack of information.

With the BBC and one or two others as the principal agents among the beneficiaries of intervention and, more or less, the sole source of information to government, 'government failure' is almost inevitable.

Peacock naturally argues for a different approach. A policy derived as far as possible from consumer preferences could be implemented by a body in receipt of hypothecated revenues, which would outline its policies and receive its bids from competitive bidders. These it would monitor, and then report on performance. Peacock acknowledges a number of problems here. He doesn't specify the performance indicators and accepts that 'quality' is difficult to measure. He also accepts that subsidy has its problems and tracking performance has its own transaction costs (the expanded Ofcom is a good example of this).

This step would, however, remove the case for retaining the BBC as a publicly financed corporation. Otherwise, as Peacock puts it, 'one perpetuates a system where the BBC is judging its own case as to what public service broadcasting means ... in which unfair competition prevails in the ability of the BBC to offer highly subsidised, commercial services made possible by, among other things, the property rights of the BBC and recorded programmes financed by the payers of the licence fee'.

Towards the end of the paper, Peacock makes important points, which, in the introverted world of broadcasting policy, have been peripheral to the argument. He is sceptical of the kind of claim made by the former BBC Chairman, Gavyn Davies, that the BBC is 'best placed to undertake the special task of preserving our national identity and self esteem, as a pre-condition for the preservation of our system of values'. The fostering of such qualities as enterprise, inventiveness, tolerance and justice are, as he puts it, 'hardly the function of a broadcasting system'. Rather, they are the function of an education system in the widest sense. Peacock would, no doubt, be hugely sceptical of the more recent claim that the BBC is a division of the welfare state, a kind of sub-set of the National Health Service. What skills have television producers got in curing national ills or diagnosing national diseases? These are issues way outside the scope of what is basically an entertainment industry with subsidiary obligations. 'Broadcasting', as Peacock puts it, is one source of knowledge and should not be 'raised to the status of a Church'.

Though he does not spell it out, I would guess from his views and from the text of his lecture that he can only really identify one absolutely clear public service role for television. That is the production of quality news and public affairs programming. Every citizen has an interest in being well informed at election time and a parallel interest in others being well informed too, since they will decide his or her future. The other aspects of public service broadcasting should be, in Peacock's view, constantly referred back for reassessment as market and consumer taste changes or a real knowledge is acquired about the effects of entertainment media on individuals and society.

# 4 COMMENTARY: WHY BROADCASTING IS STILL SPECIAL
*Carolyn Fairbairn[1]*

It is testament to the power and consistency of Professor Peacock's ideas that we are still discussing them today, nearly twenty years after the publication of his committee's seminal report on the financing of the BBC. By framing the future of broadcasting as a whole in terms of the market, the Peacock Report represented a fundamental break with all previous official reports on UK broadcasting. The report's intellectual radicalism and subsequent impact on policy have meant that much of the debate about broadcasting in recent years has been framed by a similar economic perspective.

In the BBC's view, this is the wrong starting point for a consideration of public service broadcasting and one which will result in the dismantling of the UK's successful mixed broadcasting economy. The theoretical blueprint for the future of broadcasting proposed by Peacock leads us into a trap where public service is replaced by market economics as the basis of policy decisions. In the UK, public service broadcasting is not about narrow market failure, any more than public service health and education are. It is about the collective decision we make as a society to keep some important aspects of our lives in the public realm – available to all, serving all and accountable to all. Looking ahead to the likely

---

1   Director of Strategy and Distribution, BBC. She also serves as a Managing Trustee of the IEA.

changes in our society and media markets over the next decade, we believe that public service broadcasting, and particularly the role of the BBC, will become even more, not less, important.

## Peacock's prescription

Peacock's starting point is that broadcasting is like other consumer industries and, therefore, the market, all else being equal, will deliver an optimal outcome for audiences. The last sentence of the Peacock Report stated: 'we hope to reach a position where the mystique is taken out of broadcasting and it becomes no more special than publishing became once the world became used to living with the printing press' (CFBBC, 1986). The report saw public-service-style intervention as largely a temporary response to market failure in an age of spectrum scarcity. With the transition to a fully digital world, the report's assumption was that the market would provide almost all the programming that audiences wanted and that it would do so more effectively and efficiently than public intervention. In such circumstances, public funding should be restricted to a limited amount of 'socially desirable' programming that would not otherwise be provided.

In Peacock's view, the ultimate objective of a broadcasting system is to ensure the sovereignty of the consumer. This requires subscription to be the dominant funding model, as only pay-TV enables consumer preferences to be directly expressed through the purchase of services from a range of sources of supply. Advertising funding will deliver a less efficient and desirable outcome as broadcasters do not sell programmes to audiences, but audiences to advertisers.

Peacock's original prescription for the BBC was drawn up

during the high tide of free market ideology. Then his 1986 report proposed a medium-term move to subscription funding for the BBC's television services and the establishment of a Public Service Broadcasting Council (PSBC) to fund good programming. These proposals proved politically unpalatable at the time, but major changes in UK broadcasting over the past decade have, in his view, now ushered in the conditions necessary for the creation of a market-led system. The end of spectrum scarcity and widening choice via pay-TV, so the argument goes, make radical reform of the way the BBC is financed, governed and structured essential.

The proposals outlined by Peacock in this publication were recently echoed in the report of the Elstein Commission on the future of the BBC. The commission, established by the Conservative Party, recommended that the licence fee should be progressively reduced from 2007 until its abolition at analogue switch-over, with the BBC's television services being funded largely by subscription. As with Peacock, the Elstein Report argues that public funding should in future be 'contestable' and distributed through a new intermediary to different broadcasters and producers.

It is important to note at the outset that both Peacock and Elstein exclude non-television services from their analysis. The BBC is, unlike other public service broadcasters, a tri-media organisation, and any proposed funding model must be consistent with the delivery of public service purposes by the BBC's radio and online services as well as by its television channels.

### An efficient market outcome?

Even from an economic perspective, Professor Peacock's analysis is open to question. The market alone is unlikely to deliver an economically efficient or desirable outcome for UK consumers, even after the transition to a fully digital world. This is primarily due to the enduring nature of broadcasting and the structural features of the UK market that are not easily subject to competition policy remedies.

First, the fact that programmes, once made and broadcast, can be consumed by additional viewers at zero marginal cost to the broadcaster causes problems for the market mechanism. It means that viewers may be excluded from watching a programme by the price charged even if they value it more than the cost of making it available to them. In economic terms, this would be a clear failure of the free market. In such circumstances, a universally levied flat-rate fee, along the lines of the BBC's licence fee, represents a more efficient pricing model. The BBC's licence fee delivers, for the vast majority of viewers, better value for money than pay-TV (both per month and per viewer hour; Barwise, 2004).

Second, the making and broadcasting of TV programmes continue to have exceptionally high fixed costs and very low marginal costs. The economies of scope and scale inherent in broadcasting will tend to encourage a concentration of ownership, with potential implications for viewer choice and the quality and price of available services.

Finally, the nature of a broadcaster's funding mechanism will tend to determine its programming incentives. Both economic theory and the available evidence suggest that the market, left to itself, is unlikely to provide both the high-budget domestic programming and broad range of programme types that are highly valued by UK audiences. The commercial terrestrial channels, dependent on fragmenting advertising income, may provide only the most mainstream form of programming. The UK's well-developed pay-TV sector currently invests only 3 per cent of its revenues (around £100 million per year) in original domestic content (Oliver & Ohlbaum Associates, 2003). Moreover, evidence from other countries, such as the USA, Australia and New Zealand, suggests that market-led systems tend to supply a narrower range and balance of programming than the UK's mixed broadcasting model.

So, even on grounds of economic efficiency and consumer welfare, there is a strong case to suggest that large-scale public intervention in the UK broadcasting market will continue to be necessary, even after the transition to digital.

## Public service broadcasting is not about narrow 'market failure'

Fundamentally, Peacock's analysis misunderstands the purpose of public service broadcasting and undervalues its unique contribution to virtually every aspect of our national life. This is because, in the words of Professor Steve Barnett (2004), it views the 'whole issue through the wrong end of the telescope'.

Peacock's focus on consumer economics leads him to see public service broadcasting as a narrow range of high-end genres that the market will not provide. Public service broadcasting in the USA, with its elite programming and 2 per cent audience share, is the exemplar of this 'Himalayan Heights' model. For the BBC, public service broadcasting fails in its mission if it is confined to a ghetto. It can best be described as a range of high-quality programmes and services whose overriding aim is to serve the public interest and be universally available. This reflects a choice made by successive generations to place broadcasting in the public sphere of our national life. Market economics' focus on consumer sovereignty subordinates this notion of 'social choice' and the core public principles of universality, equity and accountability that underpin it.

Fundamental choices such as these are independent of the technology of the day. The common problem with theoretical blueprints such as Peacock's is their reliance on technological determinism. There is no doubt that the growth of digital TV and convergence between platforms is changing audience behaviour and posing new challenges for broadcasting. But just because technology makes it possible to change the funding model for public service broadcasting and the BBC does not mean that it is in the public interest to do so.

Historically, the UK has put public service and cultural goals ahead of market principles in setting broadcasting policy. As a result, UK broadcasting reflects our culture, taste and values far better than in most other countries. It provides the most trusted news and information of any country in the world. The UK's mixed economy is based on a foundation of high-quality, universally available public service broadcasting free at the point of reception. In recent years, multi-channel TV has added extra choice for those willing and able to pay for more. The UK boasts the highest investment per head in domestic programmes of any country in the world, including the USA. No other country has achieved this double win of success in both public and private media.

And the lessons from outside broadcasting are also instructive. The experience of the last twenty years has shown that 'public value is best maximised neither by competitive private markets nor by monopoly public provision. Instead ... the combination of strong public sector institutions and competition from private organisations achieves the best balance of accountability, innovation and efficiency' (Kelly and Myers, 2002).

The burden of proof, therefore, rests with those such as Professor Peacock who want to dismantle the UK's broadcasting model and start all over again – but with the market replacing public service as the central organising principle. What is invariably missing in the theoretical blueprints of the kind put forward by Peacock is supporting evidence of how a market system would deliver greater value for the UK public both as consumers and citizens. Without this, we are being asked to make a gigantic leap in the dark.

## The public value of the BBC

The BBC is the cornerstone of the UK broadcasting system. While commercial broadcasters aim to create shareholder value, the BBC exists solely to maximise the public value of broadcasting by enriching the life of everyone in the UK. This means a BBC capable of broadcasting Radio 4 as well as *EastEnders*, the news as well as *The Office.* The BBC must be popular – where is the public service in being anything else? But it must achieve this popularity through providing programmes that are richer and more ambitious than those provided by the market alone.

Extending choice to all viewers and listeners is only one side of the public value equation. Of equal importance is the role that the BBC plays in enhancing the quality of life for society as a whole. The BBC's trusted and widely available news services play a pivotal role in underpinning democratic discourse in the UK, where around 70 per cent of people cite TV and radio as their main source of news. Around 90 per cent of the BBC's television output is British made and aims to provide the space for shared public conversations about who we are and what kind of society we want to live in. The BBC delivers the 'social glue' that helps bind society together at the community as well as at the national level, while also helping to bring educational opportunities to all.

There is considerable evidence that audiences themselves recognise the positive externalities created by broadcasting and believe that public service broadcasting should be drawn more widely than the proponents of narrow 'market failure' arguments would like. The extensive audience research undertaken for Ofcom's Public Service Broadcasting review, for example, reveals that sport, drama and soaps, as well as news and serious factual broadcasting, are seen as important parts of public service broadcasting, not just for the individual viewer but for their wider benefit to society.

When judged against the standards of modern public services, public service broadcasting appears to be performing rather well. The BBC is one of those rare public services that tens of millions of people choose to use every day of the week, despite exploding choice and very low switching costs. The BBC's services have massive reach: 94 per cent of the UK population currently watch and listen to the BBC across television, radio and online in any one week.

There are strong reasons for believing that, in a digital future, the value of 'publicness' in broadcasting will be even greater. As audiences fragment and industry consolidates further, the maintenance of strong, independent public service institutions will be essential if UK broadcasting is to continue delivering the quality and range of service that we value both as consumers and citizens.

Moreover, exciting new public value opportunities are emerging – access to huge archives, new ways to learn and participate in society, more local services, to name but a few – which public service broadcasters are best equipped to harness.

## The case for the licence fee

It is certainly true that subscription would allow viewers to choose whether or not to pay for and receive BBC services, and would provide a direct financial nexus between broadcaster and individual consumer. It would also fundamentally change the nature of the BBC's services, however, and the value it is able to deliver to society.

The UK public expects the BBC to be focused on serving its needs by offering a range and depth of content to everyone, regardless of ability to pay. Moreover, they value a BBC that is independent of both commercial and political influence and able to invest in high-quality and distinctive British services, programming and talent. The way in which the BBC is funded must be consistent with the achievement of these goals.

One of the major strengths of the UK's mixed broadcasting system is that the variety of funding sources – subscription, advertising and the licence fee – leads to a variety of content provision. The different content and genre mixes on BBC One as compared to ITV1 or Sky One are testament to this.

The stability of licence fee funding allows the BBC to be the standards-setter for the highest quality of public service broadcasting and to take creative risks that could not be undertaken in a commercial environment. The reality is that a BBC funded by subscription would be driven by commercial imperatives, rather than by public service and a commitment to the nation's collective welfare. Such a BBC might still have sufficient resources to make quality, popular programming, but the range of its offering would be much reduced and its distinct role in the broadcasting ecology undermined.

As the BBC sought to maximise its income from subscription and people opted out of paying, the cost of these services to everyone else would inevitably increase. This could push the cost of the BBC beyond the reach of more and more members of the public. So while subscription would give choice to some, it would progressively deny it to those who are less well off.

The licence fee remains, for the great majority of viewers, demonstrably better value for money than subscription. Those households that have chosen to subscribe to satellite or cable services pay far more for it, both per annum and per viewer-hour, than they pay for the BBC.

## The case against an 'Arts Council of the Air'

The second major plank of Peacock's analysis is that once the BBC's television services are funded via subscription, public funding should be restricted to subsidising those limited forms of programming that would not be supplied by the market. All broadcasters, including the BBC, would then be able to submit bids to a new public body for resources to make socially desirable programmes.

This approach massively underestimates the value of having strong institutions focused on public service broadcasting with the scale of creative and production resources to deliver their objectives. In many areas of our cultural and civic life, institutions play a pivotal role in sustaining public service values that risk being diluted if these institutions themselves are hollowed out. Moreover, a programme-based fund goes against the grain of public service broadcasting in the UK, which has prided itself on making programmes that are, to varying degrees, both 'good' and 'popular', rather than separating them into mutually exclusive boxes.

An independent study commissioned by the BBC outlines a number of strong arguments as to why introducing such a system into the UK would have a negative impact on net investment levels in public service content.

Far from crowding out private sector investment, the BBC plays a vitally important role in keeping UK production levels, spend and quality high across the sector. And through its size and scale, the BBC is able to make major moves that matter for the future of UK broadcasting, taking the lead where the market fails or stalls: whether it's BBC online, Freeview or DAB. Reduced investment in a range of quality and diverse content by the BBC is likely to reduce the pressure on commercial broadcasters to match its investment levels, resulting in lower quality.

There is also the real prospect that giving public money to commercial broadcasters will actually crowd out commercial investment. Pressure on commercial broadcasters from their shareholders would encourage them to bid for public funds to pay for investment that those broadcasters would have made anyway.

Dispensing public funds to all channels also raises account-ability issues. A key strength of the current licence fee is that people know what their money is paying for and who is respon-sible for delivery. The BBC is accountable to the British people for the quality of what it does, through a framework of checks and balances.

The only way to ensure 'additionality' and accountability would be through the introduction of intrusive regulation on all broadcasters which would come on top of the bureaucracy and transaction costs inherent in setting up a contestable Public Service Broadcasting Fund.

The only countries that have implemented similar systems tend to have relatively small broadcasting markets that cannot generate sufficient revenue to support home-grown quality content. And their track record is far from positive, with New Zealand currently back-pedalling from its experiment with an 'Arts Council of the Air'.

## In conclusion

The fundamental problem with Professor Peacock's analysis is that it starts in the wrong place. Market economics seriously undervalues the positive externalities created by public service broadcasting and sees its fundamental purpose as filling in the gaps left by the private sector.

Through its mass reach and influence at the heart of our daily existence, broadcasting has an unrivalled capacity to enrich people's lives as individuals as well as improve the quality of life in society as a whole. It is the recognition of this basic fact which has led us to believe that the public interest is best served by everyone having access to a range of services that deliver quality and ambitious programmes, whatever their age, sex or where they live. The British people may, at some point, choose a different approach and decide to make broadcasting primarily a private activity. But until there is convincing evidence that this is what the public wants, we should focus our collective energies on maintaining and strengthening what we already have, rather than tearing up the blueprint.

## References

Barnett, S. (2004), 'Which End of the Telescope', in *From Public Service Broadcasting to Public Service Communications*, IPPR.

Barwise, Patrick (2004), 'What are the real threats to public service broadcasting', *From Public Service Broadcasting to Public Service Communications*, IPPR, p. 20.

CFBBC (1986), *Report of the Committee on the Financing of the BBC*, Cmnd. 9824, London: HMSO (the Peacock Report).

Kelly, Gavin and Steven Myers (2002), *Creating Public Value: An Analytical Framework for Public Service Reform*, Cabinet Office, 2002.

Oliver & Ohlbaum Associates (2003), *UK Television Content in the Digital Age*.

# 5 COMMENTARY: THE FUTURE OF PUBLIC SERVICE BROADCASTING AND THE BBC

*Ed Richards and Chris Giles[1]*

## Introduction

It is hard to think of a better time to reconsider public service broadcasting and the future of the BBC. The Corporation itself is just emerging from a period of turmoil after the Hutton Report, with Michael Grade as its new Chairman and Mark Thompson as its new Director-General. The broadcasting market is going through one of its periodic technological upheavals: over half of UK homes now receive digital TV, with almost 10 per cent of homes signing up to pay for satellite TV, cable TV or free-to-view digital terrestrial TV in the past year. The government is in the middle of its review of the BBC's Royal Charter, which expires at the end of 2006. And Ofcom is undertaking its first quinquennial review of public service broadcasting.

Ofcom will publish its final report at the end of the year and has already published the Phase 1 consultation document. Phase 1 reviewed the effectiveness of public service broadcasting on the main terrestrial TV channels (BBC One, BBC Two, ITV1, Channel 4 and Five), the conceptual underpinning for public regulation and funding of certain aspects of public service TV broadcasting,

1    Ed Richards is Senior Partner of Ofcom and former senior policy adviser to the Prime Minister on media, the Internet, telecoms and e-government. Chris Giles works on policy development for Ofcom.

and some initial propositions for maintaining and strengthening public service broadcasting in the future.

We are under no illusion that everyone will agree with the review; such a feat would be impossible in broadcasting. But we hope that the evidence base will be regarded as solid, since Ofcom has commissioned more primary research than any similar previous review. Then the arguments can focus on the important issues of principle rather than on inconsequential disputes about the facts.

In relation to the principles behind public service broadcasting, few have thought for so long and so deeply as Professor Peacock. It was a great pleasure for us therefore to secure his input into our review with his stimulating paper, given at the Institute of Economic Affairs in January 2004.

Typically, Professor Peacock's paper takes a robust market-oriented view, which is long on insight and short on waffle. It reminds us of the *Report of the Committee on the Financing of the BBC* (CFBBC, 1986), which Professor Peacock chaired and which has stood the test of time. Unlike many other reports in public life, its intellectual coherence, its sharp focus on the important facts and its clarity of drafting still make it the starting point for the evaluation of public service broadcasting, whether you agree with its conclusions or not.

In some respects, we agree with Peacock. In other respects, we do not share his analysis, but we have always found it necessary to test our views against his before deriving our own initial propositions. We will first try to summarise Peacock's paper into eight proposals and discuss our Phase 1 review in that context.

## The main Peacock proposals

Professor Peacock's paper argues:

1 Any public action to influence the broadcasting system must accord with the aim of ensuring consumer sovereignty. In other words, people should be free to watch what they want to watch, without the 'guardians' of the public interest imposing their views on others. As Professor Peacock put it: 'the onus of proof is placed on government to show that the consumer interest is best achieved other than by the choices of listeners and viewers themselves'.

2 The traditional broadcasting market failure argument is relatively weak. Professor Peacock is unconvinced of this argument and argues that it 'introduces a systematic bias in favour of state intervention'. He offers the example of rediffusion, whereby entrepreneurs in the 1920s and 1930s wired extension speakers up to a radio set, but were made to operate under strict government regulation to protect the BBC monopoly. He could equally have cited the growth of subscription digital satellite and cable TV in the late 1990s, which also offered customers services they were eager to buy and which the traditional broadcasters had not offered.

3 Any intervention in favour of public service broadcasting must be aware of the dangers of government failure. These can outweigh any benefits of intervention in the market and often arise when government is acting as the principal trying to control an agent that is not subject to the disciplines of market forces.

4 There is a case for government funding of some TV broadcasting. Programmes that consumers 'wish to support,

but which they cannot expect to be provided by purely commercial operations' should receive funding if 'many listeners and viewers feel that they derive a benefit although they do not necessarily listen to or watch them'. Examples Professor Peacock cited were cultural or educational programming. Some programmes, for example, could encourage an interest in current affairs and have the potential to improve their decisions as voters.

5    There should be three pre-conditions for public funding of public service broadcasting. First, that the broadcasting market moves towards a situation where workable competition is a reality. Second, certain channels must be specified that are obliged to contain public service broadcasting: these are likely to be the main terrestrial channels but need not be in the future. Third, consideration should be given to achieving public goals through means other than broadcasting, which might not always be the best use of public funds.

6    A council should have hypothecated funds from a reformed licence fee to buy programming that meets the aims of public service broadcasting. The council would be accountable to viewers and listeners and the fund would not be for the sole use of the BBC. The level of the fund would have to be fixed ultimately by government.

7    A Public Service Broadcasting Fund would be wholly incompatible with continued BBC funding of public service broadcasting obtained from the licence fee. The big change for the BBC would be that it would no longer be able to be 'judge in its own case as to what public service broadcasting means', nor would it be able to 'offer highly subsidised

commercial services made possible, amongst other things, by the property rights of the BBC in recorded programmes financed by payers of the licence fee'.

8   Though respectable, the argument that the BBC is the broadcaster best placed to preserve our national identity and system of values is easily exaggerated. Indeed, Professor Peacock concludes by questioning whether the function of broadcasting should be to promote enterprise, inventiveness, tolerance and justice rather than it being just another tool of the broader education system. He cautions everyone not to raise broadcasting to the 'status of a Church', however broad and accommodating its presentation of moral and cultural values might be.

## An analysis of Peacock's argument

We believe the right starting point is to consider the interests of UK consumers and UK citizens, while remembering that all of us are both consumers and citizens.

As consumers, we want the TV broadcasting system to provide programming that we would pay to watch or would pay for the option to watch. As citizens, however, we also want certain programmes to be widely available for as many people as possible to watch, even if consumers would not be willing to pay enough for them to be produced and broadcast.

The duality of consumer and citizen interests creates a difficult but interesting public policy problem. In line with Peacock's first and fourth proposals, we should aim to allow consumer sovereignty to rule, subject to the provision of programming that satisfies citizens' interests. The question is how far does the current broadcasting market, with its public interventions in the form of the licence-fee-funded BBC and the obligations on ITV1, Channel 4 and Five, resemble this aim?

In the past, where spectrum was scarce and it was possible to have only a handful of TV channels, there were two main reasons why TV broadcasting did not meet consumer interests: the TV schedules in a limited-channel world would maximise income by meeting the needs of advertisers and not of viewers; and TV programmes were close to being public goods, from which people could not be excluded if they did not pay to watch a programme or a channel, and where the extra cost of broadcasting to an additional viewer was zero. Regulation of commercial TV companies and public funding were appropriate public policy responses to these twin problems.

Given the technical constraints, it is understandable that we have developed the current system of terrestrial TV. The BBC and commercial channels used all the available spectrum; the TV licence fee paid for the BBC and aimed to secure programming that otherwise would not be screened; regulation and the existence of the BBC produced a similar mix of programming on commercial channels, while some of their costs associated with less commercial programming were mitigated by subsidised access to the spectrum.

This form of funding and regulation is still relevant today, when about half the population still rely on four or five TV channels. As Peacock suggested in his second proposal, however, the consumer market failure problems described above are much weaker today than they were. They are also likely to diminish even further as digital TV reaches the vast majority of households. It is becoming increasingly clear that consumers have little to fear from a deregulated broadcasting market; with over 300 channels available, consumers will almost always be able to buy the programming they desire; and with conditional access systems readily available, they can be excluded from programmes or channels if they are not willing to pay.

The problem that TV broadcasts 'suffer' non-rivalry – that the cost to broadcasters of an extra consumer viewing their programme is zero – will remain, but many commercial businesses are successful with extremely low marginal costs (for example, the film industry, newspaper and magazine publishing and telecommunications), so this market failure does not present a strong case for intervention.

Market solutions such as bundling of programmes together into a channel, just as individual articles are bundled together in a newspaper, allow the marginal cost of any programme to be zero and significantly reduce the efficiency costs of non-rivalry. Also, as Peacock reminds us in his third proposal, the risks of government or regulatory failure are significant and the mere identification of a market failure is not sufficient ground for intervention. The net benefits of any intervention, after allowing for costs, must exceed the cost of the market failure.

We should be pleased that technology is moving us rapidly towards the point where consumers of TV broadcasts are sovereign and there is little need for intervention to secure what consumers want to watch or want the option to watch. So one of our first suggestions for the future of UK broadcasting is that a high priority should be placed on achieving digital switch-over, and this objective should be given preference over some of the current regulations imposed on commercial broadcasters.

If the market failures associated with consumer sovereignty

are diminishing, we think the same cannot be said of the ability of the TV broadcasting market to serve citizens' interests effectively. Consumer and citizens' interests diverge to the extent that some TV programmes fulfil purposes other than satisfying consumer desires.[2]

TV has a role in fulfilling social purposes desired by UK citizens. It can:

- inform us and others and increase our understanding of the world through news, information and analysis of current events and ideas;
- reflect and strengthen our cultural identity through high-quality UK, national and regional programming;
- stimulate our interest in and knowledge of arts, science, history and other topics through content that is accessible, encourages personal development and promotes participation in society; and
- support a tolerant and inclusive society through the availability of programmes that reflect the lives of different people and communities within the UK, encourage a better understanding of different cultures and perspectives and, on occasion, bring the nation together for shared experiences.

And while we should not get too overexcited about how special TV is, we should recognise that it is still the only medium that has the reach to achieve any of these aims. But Peacock is, of course, right in his eighth proposal to caution everyone against raising the status of broadcasting to that of 'a Church'.

---

2   In economic terms, some TV programmes have positive externalities or are merit goods.

With these purposes in mind, our definition of public service broadcasting is any programming that furthers these objectives. We know from our Phase 1 audience research that the public strongly supports these purposes for TV broadcasting. Though they see TV as primarily a form of entertainment, they also strongly value its role in informing us, stimulating interest in a wide range of subjects and reflecting our cultural identity. We argue that it is unlikely that the market would offer the current level of public service broadcasting, and we will test this assertion in the second phase of our review.

## Important considerations for the development of broadcasting policy

Three big questions arise from this analysis: What is the optimal level of public service broadcasting? How much will the market provide without intervention from the state? And how effective can state intervention be in securing these purposes through funding or through regulation?

Though our work in answering these questions is not complete, we have published a series of propositions for debate concerning the future of the broadcasting market as we move into a digital world.[3] Rather than list them all here, we will draw out a few of the important findings that relate to Peacock's paper.

First, we expect effective competition to develop in the broadcasting market. This is welcome, but as audiences fragment, the existing ability of commercial broadcasters to produce some elements of public service broadcasting from exploiting scarce

---

3    These can be found at <www.ofcom.org.uk>: see Ofcom (2004).

spectrum will fall. As suggested in Peacock's fifth proposal, new sources of funding should therefore be considered, which should not necessarily be limited to the existing terrestrial broadcasters. A model of contestable funding, as in Peacock's sixth proposal, is a possibility, as is a redistribution of parts of the licence fee to other broadcasters with public policy aims. These should be carefully assessed during the current year.

Second, we do not support Peacock's seventh proposal that the development of competition in broadcasting and some alternative funding for public service broadcasting are necessarily incompatible with funding the BBC from a licence fee. So long as its programming strives to meet the purposes of public service broadcasting, it creates few undesirable distortions in the broadcasting market, it is efficient, and it can retain a high audience for programmes with public service purposes, a strong publicly owned BBC would enhance the TV landscape. These are challenging conditions, but such conditions are necessary for the BBC to retain such a unique funding system.

Third, we believe that there is a strong case for there to be a plurality of providers of public service broadcasting because, if there is a lack of competition among public service broadcasting providers, the resultant market outcome is unlikely to involve high-quality public service broadcasting. Some public service broadcasting will be provided by the market, but we need to examine the case for sharing funding streams among a greater number of broadcasters and allowing broadcasters or producers to bid for public service broadcasting funding.

Fourth, we should continue to secure a substantial contribution to public service broadcasting by not-for-profit organisations in addition to contributions from profit-making broadcasters.

This is because social purposes may be more easily achieved when the organisational aims within which commissioners and schedulers work are closely aligned with public service purposes, rather than potentially in conflict with them.

And fifth, we must always recognise that the case for public funding of public service broadcasting relies on the programmes meeting public service purposes and that they are watched by sufficient numbers of people to justify the expenditure. Once digital switch-over has been achieved, public intervention to secure public service broadcasting may not be justified on its present scale, either because market failures are reduced considerably, or because it will prove impossible to secure the purposes and characteristics of public service broadcasting through television at a reasonable cost.

This is a crucial time for broadcasting. Over the next decade, we are finally likely to see the emergence of a reasonably well-functioning market in TV broadcasting. The current system of regulation and financing needs to be reformed once that market arrives, so it is the right time to consider and to begin developing an alternative.

## References

CFBBC (1986), *Report of the Committee on the Financing of the BBC*, Cmnd. 9824, London: HMSO (the Peacock Report).
Ofcom (2004), *Is Television Special?*, <http://ofcom.org.uk>.

# 6 COMMENTARY: THE SCOPE OF PUBLIC SERVICE BROADCASTING

*Stephen Pratten and Simon Deakin[1]*

*Profits, more than creative or 'democratic' impulses, are always trying to push out the boundaries on the grounds of course that this-or-that is 'what the public want' … What 'the public – we – want' should not be a first or overriding aim. There are better criteria.*

RICHARD HOGGART, 2004

## Introduction

Resources are scarce, and given the multitude and variety of potential uses to which they could be put, a mechanism is needed by which they can be allocated to particular goods and services. It is not possible to pursue all potential options. The decision to devote resources to the production of television programmes means that other options, alternative goods and services, are forsaken. Equally the provision of specific types of programming means that the possibility of supplying alternative sorts of television is denied. How is an assessment to be made between the various configurations possible? What level of resources should society devote to television and what programmes ought to be produced?

One response is to insist that alternatives should be evalu-

1   Stephen Pratten is Lecturer in Economics, King's College London. Simon Deakin is Professor of Corporate Governance, the Judge Institute, University of Cambridge.

ated according to the principle that individual consumers are the best judges of what will contribute to their own well-being. The task is then to ensure that resources are allocated so as to match, over the widest possible range, outputs to agents' wants or preferences. Those who embrace such a principle often further claim that a particular institutional arrangement, namely the market, is the most likely to generate such an outcome. The adoption of this type of framework is, of course, familiar and sometimes linked to a critical attitude towards public service broadcasting and its defenders. From this angle, while public service broadcasting may have been tolerated in an era when there were technological barriers to the formation of robust market relations, these no longer apply, and any related rationale for public service broadcasting has consequently dissolved.

Professor Peacock's position, as one would anticipate, is more complex. He adopts the principle of consumer sovereignty but maintains a positive role for public service broadcasting none the less. He questions the relevance and highlights the dangers of accounts that might mislead us into thinking that nothing more is required than for the market to be left alone. He also emphasises the advantages of 'workable competition' over futile and counter-productive attempts to reproduce a perfectly competitive equilibrium. He insists that acknowledging a role for public service broadcasting should not be confused with support for the BBC's current governance structure or existing financial and institutional arrangements. Not satisfied with offering a merely theoretical and methodological critique, Peacock is prepared to advance a sketch of the institutional implications of a public service broadcasting system based on consumer sovereignty.

In trying to understand and situate Peacock's position on

public service broadcasting it is useful to compare it with other influential contributions; in particular we will consider it in relation to the views expressed in the 1962 Pilkington Committee Report. We shall also show that the accommodation between consumer sovereignty and public purpose that Peacock recommends is very much in line with the way in which current policy debates are framed. The crucial issue remains as it did in 1960: how should we prioritise the relative benefits to be reaped from broadcasting as consumption as opposed to broadcasting as a public service? We suggest that great care is required in designing a framework within which this kind of evaluation can be made.

## Public service broadcasting and the interests of the citizen

Peacock demonstrates that even if one adopts consumer sovereignty as a guiding principle when comparing alternative regulatory and institutional possibilities, and believes that a fully fledged market system within broadcasting is finally within reach as a result of technological advances, an important role for public service broadcasting remains. This argument has, of course, already been made, in the Peacock Report on the financing of the BBC:

> The case for public support of programmes of this [public service] type can be accepted by those who believe that viewers and listeners are in the last analysis the best judges of their own interest, because:
>
> (i)  Some people may come to enjoy what they do not already as a result of new opportunities being presented.
>
> (ii) Some people will accept guidance or stimulus from

others on matters where they perceive that their knowledge or taste is limited.

(iii) Many people would like high quality material to be available even though they would not willingly watch or listen to it themselves in large enough numbers for it to be paid for directly. (CFBBC, 1986: para. 564)

The first two points here imply that while we may insist that agents always remain the *ultimate* arbiters of their own interests, they themselves may recognise that they are not the best *immediate* arbiters. This is a theme that runs through the otherwise very different contributions of the Pilkington Report of 1962, Peacock's 1986 report and the recent Ofcom review of public service broadcasting. It is, however, the third of the points quoted above which perhaps has the greatest resonance for today's debates. It involves drawing a distinction between the roles of the individual as consumer and as a citizen: 'If a full broadcasting market is eventually achieved, in which viewers and listeners can express preferences directly, the main role of public service could turn out to be the collective provision … of programmes which viewers and listeners are willing to support in their capacity of taxpayer and voters, but not directly as consumers' (ibid.: para. 580).

The kinds of considerations that influence one's decisions as a citizen may be different from the deliberations of a consumer. As a consumer we need only take account of our own preferences and do not need to defend them against the views of others. As citizens we are members of a political community and enter into a broader debate, which ultimately concerns values, about what is morally right and best for the whole community. It may be that as consumers our deliberations lead us in one direction while as citizens we are led in quite another.[2]

To illustrate: consider the example that Peacock discusses, namely a situation in which unregulated television channels compete for ratings in such a way that challenging news and current affairs programming is relegated to inaccessible slots in the schedule. Let us further suppose that this reflects the outcome of an undistorted market process based on consumers' preferences expressed through their willingness to pay. Now these same individuals may support a form of regulation that required such programming to be shown in peak time. This may be because in their role as citizens they recognise that programmes of this kind play an important part in maintaining the health of a democratic polity of the kind that enjoys general support.

If we associate public service broadcasting with the provision of material conceived of as appropriate by individuals in their role as citizens – we might speak of the *social purposes* of broadcasting in this regard – then we are characterising public service broadcasting as something different from 'consumer-oriented' broadcasting. Public service broadcasting relates to individuals not as consumers but as citizens. Giving precise content to this kind of conception of public service broadcasting has been notoriously difficult but has typically involved reference to issues of universality and quality as well as citizenship.[3] Let us put to one side the issue of what exactly these social purposes of broadcasting might be and consider the regulatory difficulties that arise as a conse-

---

2  See Keat (2000) for an interesting discussion of this issue as it relates to environmental policy.

3  For sophisticated and illuminating attempts, see Garnham (1986) and Born and Prosser (2001).

quence of adopting a conception of public service broadcasting as something other than consumer-oriented broadcasting.

One implication of accepting this position is that the regulation of broadcasting has potentially two rather distinct tasks. One role is to ensure that the interests of the consumer are protected. A second objective is to guarantee that the broadcasting system is regulated so that the benefits of public service broadcasting – the social purposes of broadcasting – are generated, thereby promoting the interests of the citizen. A central question that follows is: how much weight ought to be attached to each of these objectives? Should we prioritise the consumer or the citizen? It is important to note that this is distinct from, though it may be related to, the question of market versus public provision. If we were to place supreme priority upon the interests of the consumer then we might suppose that the market constitutes the most appropriate institutional arrangement.

To avoid the confusions caused by idealised accounts of the market, which Peacock rightly criticises, we might refer here to the interventions necessary to ensure that workable competition is established so that the interests of the 'individual as consumer' are protected. Even if one accepts the prioritisation of the consumer, however, it might be felt that for complex historical (path-dependent) reasons a situation has emerged whereby public institutions have evolved which are rather effective at matching outputs to consumer wants and therefore deserve to retain their place within a contemporary consumer-focused broadcasting ecology. The Peacock Report itself acknowledged this point (ibid.: paras. 581–3). Alternatively it might be the case that overwhelming priority is placed on securing the social purposes of broadcasting. Here a conventional assumption might be that this necessitates substantial public provision, but this needs to be argued for and not merely assumed. Before these difficult institutional issues can be broached, however, the prior question is: what weight should be attached to 'broadcasting as consumption' as opposed to the broader social purposes of broadcasting?

## Broadcasting for the consumer and the citizen

This issue gives rise to difficulties in formulating policy only if the two objectives conflict in some way. If it is the case that, perhaps as a consequence of technological advance, the conditions necessary for workable competition can now straightforwardly be established; if we assume that this is the best means of securing the consumer's interest; and if then we are satisfied that the interventions necessary to secure the additional benefits of public service broadcasting are in fact small-scale and of low cost, few dilemmas arise as a result of the existence of the two distinct objectives. It is perhaps conceivable that some means may be found by which both objectives could be secured simultaneously, in which case no choice between them nor any weighing of them would be necessary. It seems at least possible, however, that the kinds of regulatory intervention needed to promote the first objective, namely securing the interests of the consumer, may not be entirely compatible with the kinds of intervention needed to secure the second objective, that is, the social purposes of broadcasting. At the very least, once it is recognised that public service broadcasting is distinct from consumer-oriented broadcasting, the two can be seen as competing, along with other claims, for resources. The key issue that emerges is: *how much* public service broadcasting and *how much* consumer-oriented broadcasting do we need?

One way of interpreting the transformation in broadcasting policy over the last 25 years would be to see it as a move from prioritising the interests of the citizen to that of recognising the interests of the consumer *alongside* those of the citizen. In the Pilkington Report the emphasis was squarely on the social purposes of broadcasting. Thus the report considered the potential of subscription television, which even as long ago as 1962 was regarded as 'possible, because the means of metering and of access barring are now becoming available' (Committee on Broadcasting, 1962: para 972). But it did not follow that subscription television was entirely desirable. This was because the financing of broadcasting was a matter 'of constitutional significance' in so far as it affected the nature and character of broadcasting services.

Thus for Pilkington, 'the essential criterion by which to consider proposals put to us is whether services paid for in this way will, in themselves and in their effect on existing services, naturally make for the realisation of the purposes of broadcasting; or, if not naturally, can be so controlled as to ensure that those purposes will be realised' (ibid.: para 973). In similar fashion, Pilkington declined to judge commercial television by the criterion of how far it satisfied consumers' wants. Rather, like the BBC, it was there to provide 'a service which fully realises the purposes of broadcasting', and 'competition in *good* broadcasting' (emphasis added; ibid.: para 468) was the goal of policy. In this sense, there was to be no division between consumer-oriented broadcasting and public service broadcasting.

The frustration of many economists with this kind of position is well known and forcefully expressed in Ronald Coase's remarks upon the Pilkington Report:

It is easy to talk about 'the widest possible range of programme matter' but there is surely some point at which, as more and more resources are devoted to increasing the supply of programs, the gain from additional broadcast programs is of less value than the loss of value elsewhere. And if the resources devoted to broadcasting are limited in this way, it follows that the provision of programs which are liked by one group will have deprived some other group of programs that they would have liked. According to what principles is it to be decided which demands are to be satisfied? The [Pilkington] Committee never tells us this ... The Committee avoids the question of how it should be decided which programs to transmit and for the phrase 'what the public wants' they substitute another and better 'what the public authority wants'. What the public authority should want, how it would get the information which would enable it to do what it should and how in practice it would be likely to act are questions which disappear in a cloud of pious platitudes. (1966: 443–4)

A critique of this type often leads economists to conclude that any reference to the social purposes of broadcasting is at best meaningless and at worst a dangerous form of paternalism. As we have seen, however, the 1986 Peacock Report did not go this far. It brought the consumer interest to the foreground and took the advantages of the market as a starting point. But the intellectual challenge that it took up was to make sense of public service broadcasting, to understand its historical significance and to provide a rationale for its continued existence and reform. In his current contribution Peacock can again be seen as in effect taking up Coase's challenge by exploring how a regulatory agency or public authority committed to the social purposes of broadcasting might go about determining the level and deployment of resources required to deliver these broader social objectives.

It is in this spirit that Peacock now argues for a public service broadcasting fund with a formula related to the growth in overall broadcasting revenue, and proposes that the benefits of a voucher system be examined when considering the provision of public service programmes. Here Peacock seems to be suggesting that a market-like mechanism such as a voucher can be used to fulfil the broad *social* purposes of broadcasting and not just the consumer-oriented ones.

This type of intermediate stance is not unique to Peacock, but he can be seen to have initiated its use in the broadcasting policy debate. The influence of the 1986 report has indeed become remarkably widespread. At the same time, those adopting this approach have had to recognise the difficult issues of weighting and resource allocation that it inevitably raises. A striking recent example is the Ofcom review of public service broadcasting, according to which 'our social preferences as citizens may not be met by competitive market processes, even though the market might meet our private preferences as consumers' (Ofcom, 2004: 9).

## A broader framework for evaluation

This returns us to the fundamental question of how we are ulti-mately to arrive at a relative weighting of the objectives identified. How big a priority should we make 'broadcasting as consump-tion' as opposed to 'broadcasting as public service'? Both Peacock and Ofcom emphasise that value judgements are involved here. Indeed, Peacock opens his current contribution with the statement that 'this paper requires that a value judgement be made about the aim of public service broadcasting'. The Ofcom review notes that its own 'approach requires value judgements to be made about the desired role and remit of television in the UK … we need to identify what we believe to be a socially desirable outcome for television provision: there is no objective definition waiting to be picked off a shelf in the policy supermarket' (ibid.: 3). But what is implied by this emphasis upon the inevitability of value judgements?

There is a tendency for economists to espouse a form of meta-ethical scepticism, according to which all value judgements are merely the expression of individual preferences. Value judgements don't tell you anything about what they refer to, they simply express the attitudes of agents – what seems desirable to one individual need not be to another. Those who argue that value judgements are purely subjective are effectively denying the existence of any objective basis for our values – there is no independent basis on which to evaluate these judgements.[4] Once this view is adopted it encourages a very particular and, we would argue, restricted framework for the assessment of alternative policy options.

To illustrate, it is useful to draw a link here with the debates concerning the evaluative framework used to consider environmental issues. At one extreme there is a position expressed well

---

4   For discussion and criticism of this form of scepticism, see Keat, 2000, chapter 2. Peacock may not himself adopt such a position. He writes elsewhere that 'An economist need not be precluded from evaluating how individuals and governments conduct their economic affairs, but the process of evaluation requires making judgements about the "good society" which are not derived from economic analysis itself. Whether such judgements, embodying statements about human values, are themselves capable of being derived from "objective analysis", which can be submitted to scientific methods of proof, is a matter of further discussion' (Peacock, 1997: 26–7).

once more by Coase in his remarks regarding the problem of pollution:

> Like other economic problems, whether it is concerned with the supply of potatoes or houses or education, the supply of clean air or clean rivers or lakes is simply one of deciding what amount ought to be supplied, and this turns ultimately on whether what has to be given up to secure the additional supply is worth more or less than the additional supply of the commodity under discussion which it will procure. It is a matter of calculation, and it is quite possible that when the calculations are made, in general, they will show that it is better to have air, rivers and lakes which are dirtier rather than cleaner. (Coase, 1972: 313)

Now it may be that occasionally environmental policy-makers will try to broaden the scope of the calculation by attempting to take account of the ways in which people 'value' the environment beyond their immediate 'economic' relationship with it. Here it is recognised that there are not only narrowly economic but also broader social externalities to pollution. There are those who value a clean river because of its aesthetic beauty or its ability to sustain various species of fish or rare plant life and there are also those for whom the river has some value 'over and above' any contribution to their own material well-being. Sensitive economists, recognising all this but constrained by their commitment to meta-ethical scepticism, are likely to try to draw these values or 'social preferences' into some extended form of cost–benefit analysis.

It is in this vein that Ofcom's review of public service broadcasting concludes that 'there are significant commonalties' between an analysis based on market failure and one grounded in social values: both approaches 'can, in fact, be captured in a wider economic framework which considers the maximisation of social welfare, and assesses whether the market is likely to fully reflect the overall value to society of PSB'; and 'both approaches imply the need to think hard about the levers we can use to address the mismatch between what the market will provide and what society would like to secure, including the institutions entrusted with delivery' (Ofcom, 2004, supporting documents, vol. 1: 14–15).

Ofcom promises that Phase 2 of its review will involve a study of the 'costs and benefits of public service broadcasting'. Yet for social values to be included in the overall calculation of net benefits, some kind of price must be put on the preferences they are understood to represent; otherwise they will not be 'commensurate' with the more straightforwardly identifiable economic costs and benefits. This is equivalent to asking those who are potentially affected by environmental regulation how much they would be willing to pay to retain a clean river. But such exercises notoriously hit upon problems. Respondents are often resistant to the calculative approach which is implicit in this type of question: many refuse to specify any definite sum, on the grounds that the question itself is offensive to their values (see Keat, 2000: 55–6). Perhaps this is because the choice of method is not neutral. The problem with even an extended cost–benefit framework is that 'where some value is in its inherent nature not amenable to mathematical calculation, the attempt to mathematise it will almost always devalue it relative to those values that can be quantified by some agreed procedure' (Collier, 2003: 32).

## Concluding remarks

As we enter a decisive phase in the development of broadcasting policy, we are offered some hard choices over the methods used to aid us in understanding the nature and justifications for public service broadcasting. It may be that we have a choice, and that we can give greater weight to 'broadcasting as consumption' or to 'broadcasting as public service' as the case may be. What can be achieved via consumption may be so important that the 'good society' is one where broadcasting is devoted to serving the interests of individuals conceived of as isolated consumers. To privilege consumption in the absence of a wider debate over the framework of values that broadcasting policy is meant to articulate and promote, however, would be highly problematic. We have moved so far from the supposed elitism of the Pilkington Report that 'common sense' dictates that consumption be given priority, but the wisdom of this has yet to be established on any convincing basis.

## References

Born, G. and T. Prosser (2001), 'Culture and Consumerism: Citizenship, Public Service Broadcasting and the BBC's Fair Trading Obligations', *Modern Law Review*, 64(5).

CFBBC (1986), *Report of the Committee on the Financing of the BBC*, Cmnd. 9824, London: HMSO (the Peacock Report).

Coase, R. H. (1966), 'The Economics of Broadcasting and Government Policy', *American Economic Review*, 56.

Coase, R. H. (1972), comment on 'The Muted Voice of the Consumer in Regulatory Agencies', in W. J. Samuels and H. M. Trebing (eds), *A Critique of Administrative Regulation of Public Utilities*, Michigan Institute of Public Utilities.

Collier, A. (2003), *In Defence of Objectivity*, London: Routledge.

Collins, R. (2003), 'The BBC – Too Big, Too Small or Just Right',
   *Political Quarterly*, 74 (2).

Committee on Broadcasting (1962), *Report of the Committee
   on Broadcasting 1960*, Cmnd. 1753, London: HMSO (the
   Pilkington Report).

Garnham, N. (1986), 'The Media and the Public Sphere', in P.
   Golding, G. Murdock and P. Schlesinger, *Communicating
   Politics: Mass Communications and the Political Process*,
   Leicester University Press.

Hoggart, R. (2004), *Mass Media in a Mass Society*, London:
   Continuum.

Keat, R. (2000), *Cultural Goods and the Limits of the Market*,
   London: Macmillan.

Ofcom (2004), *Is Television Special?*, <http://ofcom.org.uk>.

Peacock, A. (1997), *The Political Economy of Economic Freedom*,
   Cheltenham: Edward Elgar.

Peacock, A. (2000), 'Market Failure and Government Failure in
   Broadcasting', *Economic Affairs*, December.

# ABOUT THE IEA

The Institute is a research and educational charity (No. CC 235 351), limited by guarantee. Its mission is to improve understanding of the fundamental institutions of a free society with particular reference to the role of markets in solving economic and social problems.

The IEA achieves its mission by:

- a high-quality publishing programme
- conferences, seminars, lectures and other events
- outreach to school and college students
- brokering media introductions and appearances

The IEA, which was established in 1955 by the late Sir Antony Fisher, is an educational charity, not a political organisation. It is independent of any political party or group and does not carry on activities intended to affect support for any political party or candidate in any election or referendum, or at any other time. It is financed by sales of publications, conference fees and voluntary donations.

In addition to its main series of publications the IEA also publishes a quarterly journal, *Economic Affairs*.

The IEA is aided in its work by a distinguished international Academic Advisory Council and an eminent panel of Honorary Fellows. Together with other academics, they review prospective IEA publications, their comments being passed on anonymously to authors. All IEA papers are therefore subject to the same rigorous independent refereeing process as used by leading academic journals.

IEA publications enjoy widespread classroom use and course adoptions in schools and universities. They are also sold throughout the world and often translated/reprinted.

Since 1974 the IEA has helped to create a world-wide network of 100 similar institutions in over 70 countries. They are all independent but share the IEA's mission.

Views expressed in the IEA's publications are those of the authors, not those of the Institute (which has no corporate view), its Managing Trustees, Academic Advisory Council members or senior staff.

Members of the Institute's Academic Advisory Council, Honorary Fellows, Trustees and Staff are listed on the following page.

The Institute gratefully acknowledges financial support for its publications programme and other work from a generous benefaction by the late Alec and Beryl Warren.

99

Other papers recently published by the IEA include:

## WHO, What and Why?

*Transnational Government, Legitimacy and the World Health Organization*
Roger Scruton
Occasional Paper 113; ISBN 0 255 36487 3
£8.00

## The World Turned Rightside Up

*A New Trading Agenda for the Age of Globalisation*
John C. Hulsman
Occasional Paper 114; ISBN 0 255 36495 4
£8.00

## The Representation of Business in English Literature

Introduced and edited by Arthur Pollard
Readings 53; ISBN 0 255 36491 1
£12.00

## Anti-Liberalism 2000

*The Rise of New Millennium Collectivism*
David Henderson
Occasional Paper 115; ISBN 0 255 36497 0
£7.50

## Capitalism, Morality and Markets

Brian Griffiths, Robert A. Sirico, Norman Barry & Frank Field
Readings 54; ISBN 0 255 36496 2
£7.50

## A Conversation with Harris and Seldon

Ralph Harris & Arthur Seldon
Occasional Paper 116; ISBN 0 255 36498 9
£7.50

## Malaria and the DDT Story

Richard Tren & Roger Bate
Occasional Paper 117; ISBN 0 255 36499 7
£10.00

## A Plea to Economists Who Favour Liberty: Assist the Everyman

Daniel B. Klein
Occasional Paper 118; ISBN 0 255 36501 2
£10.00

## The Changing Fortunes of Economic Liberalism

*Yesterday, Today and Tomorrow*
David Henderson
Occasional Paper 105 (new edition); ISBN 0 255 36520 9
£12.50

## The Global Education Industry

*Lessons from Private Education in Developing Countries*
James Tooley
Hobart Paper 141 (new edition); ISBN 0 255 36503 9
£12.50

## Saving Our Streams

*The Role of the Anglers' Conservation Association in*
*Protecting English and Welsh Rivers*
Roger Bate
Research Monograph 53; ISBN 0 255 36494 6
£10.00

## Better Off Out?

*The Benefits or Costs of EU Membership*
Brian Hindley & Martin Howe
Occasional Paper 99 (new edition); ISBN 0 255 36502 0
£10.00

## Buckingham at 25

*Freeing the Universities from State Control*
Edited by James Tooley
Readings 55; ISBN 0 255 36512 8
£15.00

## Lectures on Regulatory and Competition Policy

Irwin M. Stelzer

Occasional Paper 120; ISBN 0 255 36511 X

£12.50

## Misguided Virtue

*False Notions of Corporate Social Responsibility*

David Henderson

Hobart Paper 142; ISBN 0 255 36510 1

£12.50

## HIV and Aids in Schools

*The Political Economy of Pressure Groups and Miseducation*

Barrie Craven, Pauline Dixon, Gordon Stewart & James Tooley

Occasional Paper 121; ISBN 0 255 36522 5

£10.00

## The Road to Serfdom

*The* Reader's Digest *condensed version*

Friedrich A. Hayek

Occasional Paper 122; ISBN 0 255 36530 6

£7.50

**Bastiat's *The Law***
Introduction by Norman Barry
Occasional Paper 123; ISBN 0 255 36509 8
£7.50


**A Globalist Manifesto for Public Policy**
Charles Calomiris
Occasional Paper 124; ISBN 0 255 36525 X
£7.50


**Euthanasia for Death Duties**
*Putting Inheritance Tax Out of Its Misery*
Barry Bracewell-Milnes
Research Monograph 54; ISBN 0 255 36513 6
£10.00


**Liberating the Land**
*The Case for Private Land-use Planning*
Mark Pennington
Hobart Paper 143; ISBN 0 255 36508 X
£10.00

### IEA Yearbook of Government Performance 2002/2003
Edited by Peter Warburton
Yearbook 1; ISBN 0 255 36532 2
£15.00


### Britain's Relative Economic Performance, 1870–1999
Nicholas Crafts
Research Monograph 55; ISBN 0 255 36524 1
£10.00


### Should We Have Faith in Central Banks?
Otmar Issing
Occasional Paper 125; ISBN 0 255 36528 4
£7.50


### The Dilemma of Democracy
Arthur Seldon
Hobart Paper 136 (reissue); ISBN 0 255 36536 5
£10.00

## Capital Controls: a 'Cure' Worse Than the Problem?

Forrest Capie
Research Monograph 56; ISBN 0 255 36506 3
£10.00

## The Poverty of 'Development Economics'

Deepak Lal
Hobart Paper 144 (reissue); ISBN 0 255 36519 5
£15.00

## Should Britain Join the Euro?

*The Chancellor's Five Tests Examined*
Patrick Minford
Occasional Paper 126; ISBN 0 255 36527 6
£7.50

## Post-Communist Transition: Some Lessons

Leszek Balcerowicz
Occasional Paper 127; ISBN 0 255 36533 0
£7.50

## A Tribute to Peter Bauer

John Blundell et al.
Occasional Paper 128; ISBN 0 255 36531 4
£10.00

## Employment Tribunals

*Their Growth and the Case for Radical Reform*

J. R. Shackleton

Hobart Paper 145; ISBN 0 255 36515 2

£10.00

## Fifty Economic Fallacies Exposed

Geoffrey E. Wood

Occasional Paper 129; ISBN 0 255 36518 7

£12.50

## A Market in Airport Slots

Keith Boyfield (editor), David Starkie, Tom Bass & Barry Humphreys

Readings 56; ISBN 0 255 36505 5

£10.00

## Money, Inflation and the Constitutional Position of the Central Bank

Milton Friedman & Charles A. E. Goodhart

Readings 57; ISBN 0 255 36538 1

£10.00

## railway.com
*Parallels between the early British railways and the ICT revolution*
Robert C. B. Miller
Research Monograph 57; ISBN 0 255 36534 9
£12.50


## The Regulation of Financial Markets
Edited by Philip Booth & David Currie
Readings 58; ISBN 0 255 36551 9
£12.50


## Climate Alarmism Reconsidered
Robert L. Bradley Jr
Hobart Paper 146; ISBN 0 255 36541 1
£12.50


## Government Failure: E. G. West on Education
Edited by James Tooley & James Stanfield
Occasional Paper 130; ISBN 0 255 36552 7
£12.50


## Waging the War of Ideas
John Blundell
Second edition
Occasional Paper 131; ISBN 0 255 36547 0
£12.50

## Corporate Governance: Accountability in the Marketplace
Elaine Sternberg
Second edition
Hobart Paper 147; ISBN 0 255 36542 X
£12.50

## The Land Use Planning System
*Evaluating Options for Reform*
John Corkindale
Hobart Paper 148; ISBN 0 255 36550 0
£10.00

## Economy and Virtue
*Essays on the Theme of Markets and Morality*
Edited by Dennis O'Keeffe
Readings 59; ISBN 0 255 36504 7
£12.50

## Free Markets Under Siege
*Cartels, Politics and Social Welfare*
Richard A. Epstein
Occasional Paper 132; ISBN 0 255 36553 5
£10.00

## Unshackling Accountants

D. R. Myddelton

Hobart Paper 149; ISBN 0 255 36559 4

£12.50

## The Euro as Politics

Pedro Schwartz

Research Monograph 58; ISBN 0 255 36535 7

£12.50

## Pricing Our Roads

*Vision and Reality*

Stephen Glaister & Daniel J. Graham

Research Monograph 59; ISBN 0 255 36562 4

£10.00

## The Role of Business in the Modern World

*Progress, Pressures and Prospects for the Market Economy*

David Henderson

Hobart Paper 150; ISBN 0 255 36548 9

£12.50

To order copies of currently available IEA papers, or to enquire about availability, please contact:

Lavis Marketing
IEA orders
FREEPOST LON21280
Oxford OX3 7BR

Tel: 01865 767575
Fax: 01865 750079
Email: orders@lavismarketing.co.uk


The IEA also offers a subscription service to its publications. For a single annual payment, currently £40.00 in the UK, you will receive every title the IEA publishes during the course of a year, invitations to events, and discounts on our extensive back catalogue. For more information, please contact:

Subscriptions
The Institute of Economic Affairs
2 Lord North Street
London SW1P 3LB

Tel: 020 7799 8900
Fax: 020 7799 2137
Website: www.iea.org.uk